Break the Chains

By Pachino Williams

Cover Painted by Jillian Williams

Created by Jazzy Kitty Publications

Logo Designs by Andre M. Saunders/Leroy Grayson

Editor: Anelda L. Attaway

© 2021 Pachino Williams

ISBN 978-1-954425-26-2

Library of Congress Control Number: 2021911330

All rights reserved. This book is protected by the copyright laws of the United States of America. This book may not be copied or reprinted for commercial gain or profit. The use of short quotations or occasional page copying for personal or group study is permitted and encouraged. Permission will be granted upon request for Worldwide Distribution. Printed in the United States of America. Published by Jazzy Kitty Publishing utilizing Microsoft Publishing Software and Bookcover Pro. The Holy Scriptures are from the Holy Bible.

ACKNOWLEDGMENTS

I acknowledge God and my children.

DEDICATIONS

This book is dedicated to my parents: Aldrena and Bobby Williams.

To my children: Samaria, Emani, Jahhlive, and Kayla.

To my siblings: Shannon, Brodrick, and Qubia.

To my nephews: Daishawn and Shannon Jr.

The Williams family, the Anderson family, the Griffin family, the Rauls family, and the Smith family.

This book is my gift to the world, the African American culture, and future generations.

TABLE OF CONTENTS

INTRODUCTION……………………………………………..i
CHAPTER 1 – The Awakening……………………………….01
CHAPTER 2 – Africa Calling………………………………..11
    Vocation…………………………………………... 11
    The Mother Land……………………………………. 15
    African Pride………………………………………… 20
CHAPTER 3 – Royalty……………………………………….29
    The Historians………………………………………..29
    King's………………………………………………...33
    Queen's……………………………………………… 38
    The King's Set Sail………………………………….. 42
    The Moor's…………………………………………..44
    African World………………………………………. 46
CHAPTER 4 – The Invaders………………………………… 54
    The Divide…………………………………………... 54
    Servitude……………………………………………. 60
CHAPTER 5 – Slave Boat's Docking………………………... 72
    Deportation…………………………………………. 72
    Slavery……………………………………………… 74
CHAPTER 6 – America ……………………………………..82
    Necessity…………………………………………….. 82
    Foundation…………………………………………... 90
    Liberation…………………………………………….97
CHAPTER 7 – Slavery's Aftermath…………………………..102
    Migration……………………………………………..102

TABLE OF CONTENTS

Population Control..103
Smoke Screen..113
New Beginnings..115
CHAPTER 8 – Freedom Fighters..119
    The Desirables..119
    The Undesirables..124
CHAPTER 9 – New Day..130
    The White Man's New Trick...130
    New Slavery..134
CHAPTER 10 – The Chains..139
    The Placing (Cause)...139
    The Removal (The Effects)..144
CHAPTER 11 - Solutions..150
    Man..150
    Woman...153
    The World..156
Last Thoughts..163
ABOUT THE AUTHOR..167
REFERENCES..168

INTRODUCTION

Break the Chains is a breathtaking view from a narrative never seen before. The author takes you directly to the playing field of systemic racism in present-day America, which gives you a frightening peek inside our past, present, and future. This book follows the author's attempt to find himself while inside America's greatest game, the prison system. Through his own life view of seeing the educational system, judicial system, and prison system fail then funnel himself and thousands of others inside modern-day slavery.

Break the Chains serves as a blueprint and a historical source of facts collected worldwide. Strictly a guide to those eager to know the history and truth, only knowledge can reveal as he searches for culture, religion, self-gratification, and justice as a Black American male in America.

This book reveals the smoke screens and pitfalls that have been placed in his life and the lives of all African American's. Breaking the chains of our never-ending struggle for freedom, equality and financial acceptance in America.

Break the Chains

CHAPTER 1

AWAKENING

From early controversy to greatness through suffrage, adversity, and a wide variety of growing pains. The new American Negro was bred out of deception, poverty, and pain. Amazingly we as African Americans still thrived through all of our struggles. How? Because we have always clung tightly to a small sense of pride. Painstakingly Mentally, these global injustices left the American African with a low moral justification of reality and a twisted definition of pride. The new slave has been taught that the system was fixed, cleaned up, and purified of its racism and hatred. If this was the case, then great, yet still, we as a people have yet to heal mentally, which is evident through today's political, social, and law enforcement issues.

We have yet to realize that their fear and hatred also bring pure admiration. This admiration quietly reveals the secret fear. Fear of our natural talents, knowledge, physical structure, and royal heritage. I strongly feel that the false teachings and outrageous actions of this generation were guided deliberately. This thought is not a mirage; I soon found the facts. I found out that my thoughts of freedom and equality remain a misdirection of our reality as African Americans. A hologram! I realized that they gave us so much to keep us docile, subservient, and blinded. The pricey clothes, jewelry, mentally unproductive music, rims simply said bullshit! Then they pushed drugs, alcohol, and many other distractions into our communities. This action's reaction was ultimately keeping our minds docile, non-cohesive, and misdirected. A smoke screen!

It's no coincidence that today's generation is focused on keeping up with the Kardashian's, gang banging, snitching, and a farfetched rapper lifestyle. The old cliche of crabs in the barrel is real! The Willie Lynch letter on how to make a slave is real! The sad reality is it has been this way since African Americans first plights for freedom.

W.E.B. Dubois once relayed to Charles Mowbry, a White newspaper reporter that, *"Marcus Garvey was a demagogue, whose movement would collapse in a short time, and that his followers are the lowest type of Negro mostly from the west indies."* This statement from another African American fighting for his freedom is lunacy to me! Mainly because Marcus Garvey believed that. "Our failings in the past, present, and future will be through our failure to know ourselves and to realize the true functions of racism, slavery, and hatred." Did W.E.B. Dubois not know the purest, unbreakable, and strongest enslaved Africans landed in the West Indian islands first! Did he not know the majority of the subservient and docile ones became American slaves or was he just being subservient himself?

The question is, to who was he serving? He, like most, is unknowingly serving America's plans by pulling the next African down just as he did in his interview! Ironically, how was it that Garvey and these West Indians still unbreakable and speaking up for all Africans? How was it that they were more outraged than we were about our treatment as Africans in the United States? They were at this time more vigilant in our fight for American equality. How? We were too busy with capitalistic toys, drugs, clothes, etc. In my theory, the silent American Negro is the lowest type of Negro. Why? Because even then, most just stood idol and today are still standing idol. While the outspoken Negro dies and takes the heat. With that being said, it was not intended to hurt anyone who has done anything to help any oppressed people prevail over injustice. That statement was for everyone who is quick to complain, judge, and downgrade other's work when all the while doing nothing.

Black people as a whole for centuries have had their foot on each other's neck for far too long in America. Still today, we have people like Al Sharpton, Deloris Tucker, and even the president. Donald Trump was complaining about the youths sounding of the alarms of the ghetto and housing projects. Urban music groups like NWA, Public Enemy, Dead President, or rappers like Tupac, Nipsey Hustle, Common, Jezzy, Bossie, Sauce Walka, BOB, etc. Tell the stories of the outrage and pains of the ghetto. Singers like Marvin Gaye, Billy holiday, Alicia Keys, Beyonce, H.E.R., and Ericka Badu tell the story of broken people. They reveal the effects of slavery leftovers through their lyrics. Problems that we live with and deal with even today. Issues like widespread police brutality, child pregnancy, rape, drug use, and a host of other Governmental assisted plans to silently destroy us!

Sadly, with transatlantic slavery, African Americans lost their culture. Even more detrimental is the fact that most African Americans don't know or even care. Unlike any race on this planet, the American Negro has been the worst treated. Long before Booker T. Washington's and W.E.B. Dubois's racial debates, Martin Luther King's and Malcolm X's opposing views on race or war. The African American culture, religion, and people have been misled and divided. Long before the deaths of Trayvon Martin, Medgar Evers, George Floyd, or the Federal infiltration of the Black Panthers in California. We have been divided! Most don't understand that freeway Ricky Ross's betrayal was not his plan, but our governments. We as a people have to overstand that to mentally grasp this completely. We have to go back to where the divide first started. In Africa!

Plainly stated, everyone knows that without knowledge of who we are and where we are from, we as a people are lost. We will simply never see why. They (the oppressors) or us (the oppressed.) Think as we do mentally. This mental digging for oneself also exposes the smoke screens and lies of the oppressed in our history and bloodlines.

For example, slavery's origin. Slavery didn't start in Africa or just with Africans. In history's truth, every race, religion, and culture has been a subservient race at one point in history. Every race since humanity's existence. Some may think it's crazy, yet by nature's law, it is justified. The first law of mankind was the strong over power the weak! Still, sadly without servitude, not slavery, we wouldn't have Egypt, Memphis, Rome, London, or the great United States. Better stated any major civilization in history. Don't get me wrong; I'm not saying that servitude is Ok. I am saying that in the past, servant, or people of servitude was normal. Still, the servants had rights! Servitude even exists today and is still a major economical factor in third-world countries and major ones. Places like Indonesia, Bangladesh, or China, all places with a heavily divided economical class or cast system, and lax child labor laws exploit the weak to benefit the United States and other world powers.

Unknowingly the Black race in the United States today are still in servitude. Economically! What's baffling is ninety percent don't even know it. It is willingly given in exchange for financial advancement and taken for the same reason as today's servitude. This well-structured system is hidden in some instances or cloaked in such a way you would have to dig to even realize it. This digging is done through knowledge! Some have found it, yet the majority is still blinded to it. Let's take a quick second and slow down before discussing economics and letting go back to 1619.

In 1619 the first documented slaves arrived in America. History since then has shown that Africans have been un mistakenly instrumental in the forging of the United States without a doubt. Contrary to America's history books which downplay this fact. Africans were the backbone of this country! Still, with the people with books' poisoning, they strategically have compelled vigorously upon the African American youth. Books that portray us in a minuscule light, as savages, unintelligent servants, are all to suppress your talents, pride, and growth, positively without the Black, Red, and Yellow men servitude. The great United States would have never made it to existence! Let alone thrived to become the great behemoth that it is today.

Europeans have stood on someone else backs, from the Native Americans' compassionate yet naive ways to the first slave boat docking. The Indians should have never spared the English. Yet they did by simply not letting them starve. They showed compassion by teaching them to hunt and grow crops. They did not treat the English as slaves or inferior. Then the English rewarded them with plagues, slaughters, and finally reservations which equal 1% of the land they once called home.

Let's not forget the use of the Chinese, Africans, and Irish, which constructed the great railroads, or the slaves that worked the never-ending cotton fields in Georgia. The children that worked the steel mines in Alabama or the cane fields in Louisiana. African Americans have helped pave the way in many ways. From the slaver's hands in Africa to the overseers' watchful eye in the Carolinas. Millions of Kings, Queens, Princes, and Chiefs were brought to this island, shackled in bondage. Painstakingly chained for months at a time, trafficked in an area the size of a coffin. Chained to the dying!

Let's take a moment if you will, and I will try to paint a picture for you. Imagine a rat the size of a small house cat scrounging these slave ships. The rat gnawing on the dead and the living alike. You cannot move to simply brush them away! So hungry, exhausted you want to die! Tired of even screaming about the pain as they bite off your toes and fingers. Let's imagine young African princes being walked miles barefoot to the African coastline for deportation. During this trip, she was raped multiple times at each stop. She was raped to the point that she would rather keep walking on those bare bloody feet than to stop. Her soul torn, pride stolen, and a bloodline broken! She knew that at every stop, the sexual assaults would come. Still more appalling is the fact that young African men were also raped! If it were to install fear, or to most, this tactic was just a sick homosexual fulfillment. Either way, it was crazy! Try to picture a young African male prince, never knowing a homosexual person in his life. In a land of thousands of languages, yet knowing no words for homosexual or gay, English words! Picture him being violently attacked sexually by grown men! Attacked to the point where he cannot stand, sit, or walk. This future king's mentally now broken, not wanting to live to the next day. These horrific details are all facts yet vastly overlooked atrocities because these rapes were done in public, in eyeshot, or in earshot of his brothers, friends, uncle, father, or mother. All done in by the Dutch, Portuguese, French, and English under the watchful eye of the catholic church. Painstakingly then, our ancestors were shipped like animals to a new land with new sounds, people, religion, and even given new names. Instead of Sabir, Mustafa, or Malik. (thankful, strong, and King) They were given names like Toby, Sam, and Frank. Names without meaning, names without honor, or their history and bloodline. They now were lowly servants, lower than a horse, donkey, or cow someone's property.

It was a story of an African slave girl who had gotten stolen by a White man who wasn't her owner. The man's name was (Robert Hoffman). When he was sentenced for his crime, he got three years for the woman, and four years for a stolen horse he was also in possession of. Can someone explain how in America, the land of the free, a so-called Christian and civilized land? A horse is worth more than human life. In every religious text and book, God's teachings state that man was in charge of all the animals on this earth. Not lesser or equal. I guess God's opinion didn't matter when it came to Africans, or they really thought we were animals. The irony in this story was that in the same breath, an time. These Europeans were enslaving millions. They themselves were fighting for their liberation from England. Simultaneously they laid a plan and started oppressing a whole different race of people. Baffling, isn't it! The American Indian first, then the African.

The latter was treated more harshly and savagely than anyone on this planet. Abigail Adams, President John Adam's wife, said, "It always appeared most iniquitous scheme to her for them to fight for freedom when they were taking freedom away from people that have just as much right to freedom as they do." Realistically how can a race of civilized people have peace knowing the effects of and pains that their actions would have on that race in the future? Let me answer that for you. They didn't care! Today if you look deep into society's problems, you will find the effects of the chains, not just in African Americans but in White Americans also. Let me explain deeper. The European bloodline got so used to mistreatment, rapes, and other deviant sexual acts on unwilling participants. That today their offspring are now the main benefactors and violators in America. With child molestation, rape, etc. Again, Shockingly they still receive less jail and prison time for these savage acts. At the same time, minority drug dealers, robbers, and petty thieves fund the prison system. Astonishing yet true!

As for African Americans, the effects from the chains are widespread. The youth hate each other so quickly before they even speak to each other. The light-skinned hate the dark skin. The northern Blacks hate, the southern Blacks, and the east hates the west. All The effects of the dark field hands manipulated hatred for the lighter-skinned house servants. Effects of the chains! American slavery created a blatant lack of culture and pride in being dark-skinned. Direct effects of the chains! Effects of years of slavery! Instead of empowering each other, we look for faults first to bring them down. What if only we helped, loved, and taught one another
first. What if we had more pride in being Black, being African?

Maybe then he or she grows up in that poverty-stricken society. Could still provide for the next. In turn, producing a society with Blacks real Blacks in power. Real power! That simple process will help the race as a whole and ultimately help the world. A baffling fact is that we, as a people, Black Americans have no culture. "Culture" meaning like the Chinese, German, Mexican, African, etc. Meaning they eat Mexican food, dress Chinese, have German traditions. Now ask yourself what African American

Break the Chains

Culture is? Let me guess soul food, the Blues, Rap, gold teeth, twerking, Biggie and Tupac. First off, no offense to Tupac, whom I believe helped spark the first lights in my brain and many more Black American youths about injustice with his realness of ghetto life. Tupac was a teacher, and through his music, me and millions of others learned a lot! It's boldly still evident that we as African Americans, don't have a culture.

It's baffling because we think we are moving forward with a few expensive houses, clothes, jewels, and cars. Where? I ask into the European system or our own. I ask you with all this police brutality, voter suppression, child pregnancy, abortion, and drug use. This doesn't seem forward to me. Let me tell you Where we have gotten. We, as African Americans, are at a low level of European capitalism, which is crazy! With all that American Africans have been through, we are still where we started. In chains!

I sat one day when I was in prison and watched different races interact with each other. The Spanish people bonded and loved each other no matter what gang affiliation, financial situation, or geographical area they came from. They all stuck together; it was the same with the Whites, Asians, and Indians. I also observed that without knowing each other, the Blacks hated each other. They despised each other for the smallest craziest reason. Some reasons so juvenile a child could see past these petty differences. I thought to myself; this was crazy! I thought about myself growing up, and yes, without knowledge. I was once a blinded youth doing the same bullshit! I realized that back then, I found myself blindly following the effects of the chains and hating my own people, the same as them. It was only until I grew mentally, spiritually, and learned historically who I was that I began to change. I felt proud to be who I was! I learned that to gain strength. My people had to break the chains of the past! This plan ultimately not just freeing ourselves mentally, but freeing others also. Teaching the ones that don't even see the chains. Freeing them by simply educating them and opening their eyes.

    I hope and pray this book removes all the blinders from my brother's and sister's eyes. I pray my thoughts and words make us strive to uplift the African spirit, love, and community. This change is affecting not only the cities but the whole USA. Then with that strength, just maybe we will help the docile, poverty-stricken areas in our motherland. Africa! Don't get me wrong, I know this mission won't be easy, but if accomplished. It would be worth more than all the gold and riches in this crazy world. Buy simply put, "Reaching one and teaching one" This knowledge then snowballing, and ultimately breaking the chains!

CHAPTER 2
AFRICA CALLING

<u>VOCATION</u>

I remember getting shipped from Smith State Prison in Georgia to a privately-owned prison run by a C.C.A company. When I arrived at this prison/warehouse, I found myself thinking. Damn! Have I just gotten sold like a slave! This left me lost, pondering, and upset, thinking, do I belong to someone? That situation and many others in my life made me realize that I did belong to someone. America! With that knowledge, I started searching for reasons on how I started asking myself questions. How did I get here? Where did Malcolm, Martin, Marcus, and Nat go wrong?

Most importantly me! Where did I go wrong as an African American male? I weighed my good and bad throughout my own life. Mentally checking to see if I deserved this situation. Honestly, it still felt wrong for me as a Black male in 2017, defending myself to now be sold. Still to now belong to someone.

The following next days. I felt lifeless by realizing mentally that I was someone's property! I thought to myself; this is crazy! Decades after slavery's chains, I was still a commodity. I felt like an animal, livestock. I thought, how? In 2017 after slavery supposedly had been abolished, peonage dismantled, and the Black codes lifted. This was lifetimes after the Trans-Atlantic routes were closed; they still were profiting off my bloodline. That day I felt strongly that some were I was making someone money. I was making someone rich! Rich off my suffering and troubles. I felt off now, mentally disturbed. Being housed with thousands of others like livestock. As weeks passed, the thoughts got worst. The hunger grew stronger! I had to find out how! I awoke one night at 2:00 am startled and sweating from a horrible dream. I was chained on the bottom of a slave ship in that dream, and a rat was eating on my toes. I yelled but couldn't move because I was chained to the boat. I screamed, waking up! That night scared me. All the while it, awakened me mentally and spiritually. I realized symbolically I was on a boat for real. I felt anger and hate now. I was lost thinking how in the world this system could still be holding me in chains. Soon I started to look for the issues that held me in chains. The more I read, I could hear my ancestors yelling! Help us! Loud and clear. That day I realized I still was a slave, just in a different time. I realized that C.C.A. was getting rich, that I was being traded on the stock market, and more. The next day I sat on my bed thinking about the dream. Looking around the dorm room calmly. I started staring at all the bunk beds and all the people being housed in this warehouse-like livestock. I felt fear because this wasn't just happening in Georgia. This was going on all across the united states. I thought to myself; someone is getting major paid! Someone was living lavishly and making a life by keeping me confined illegally. With time and research, I found out thousands of Blacks and Hispanics are systematically imprisoned in the United States. Incarceration numbers twice as much as some in other countries and triple in some.

Unfortunately, I've been behind these walls, and I've seen firsthand the treatment and fright in these young males' faces. Fear even after a life of crime and hardships, most are already disadvantaged in a system that's rigged. Rigged how? Being a Black man in America, you are always behind. First, you receive minimal education. Then minimal health care. If you somehow break one of their laws, you receive minimal legal assistance and succumb to a high plea bargain rate for the judicial system. Then you are back in slavery's grips. Most don't realize it and let the government-assigned lawyer sell you out instead of learning the system and trying to fight for your lives. Take my word for it. I've been there. I've made those mistakes, and it cost me decades of my life. It's crazy fighting a racist, capitalistic system. A system that is designed already for them to lose. A system added by our presidents, lawmakers, and even Black political leaders. These horrific obstacles are facts and not a figment of mine or the two-point three million incarcerated African Americans' imagination.

One out of three African males will go to prison, jail, or be put on probation or parole in America. Thus wedging ourselves deeper into a system that makes the oppressors more money. That day I wondered did my ancestors have the same fright in their eyes. The same fear, pain, and feeling of being lost! How did they feel when they were taken, sold, and tricked. Whatever way you choose to put it. I wonder where they were scared when they got sold on the auction blocks in these foreign countries to enslavement. I wondered for days, so I started looking for answers. Horrifically as I read more and discovered more, I learned they were frightened, scared, confused, and beyond contemplation. What I also learned, most importantly, though. They were African; they fought, and they were brave!

Since my adolescent years, I've always felt trapped for some reason. Trapped With my destiny held back from greatness, knowledge, and learning. I finally realized why; I realized that it was simply because I was culturally confused. I was an African first, then an American, or was I an American than African. If so, as an African, I knew nothing about Africa.

And truthfully, nothing about the real America. Since my youth, I've always wanted to know about Africa. This hunger, this secret quest, was not at all sparked by my ambitions. I want to give all the credit for this hunger to my mother. Miss Aldrena Williams, she gave me my first thoughts and desires to learn. To find out all I could about being African. My mother always motivated me as a child to watch positive African History shows, movies, and culture. She told me stories of my Royalty and Uniqueness. She just keeps me involved in the learning period. So, I read great poems, books, and history written by intelligent, motivated, strong African people. Eventually, I started a strong love affair with Africa.

A love that with time only grew stronger and still exists. It blazes in my mind today more powerful simply because of gained knowledge. When I was a youth, I loved to watch TV, movies anything about Africa. TV shows like Roots, Shaka Zulu, Hell, even the impossible Tarzan. In these shows, they showed a different Africa. This wasn't the Africa that I read in books. The tv showed Africans as violent savages. A different Africa that I loved. The Africans I loved in books like Uncle Toms Cabin, Dark water, African Fundamentalism, or Negro History were different. These books and people I thought were amazing, with their strong values and habits. These books motivated me to win tremendously. Men like Malcolm X, Marcus Garvey, and Carter G. Wilson. Great poets like Maya Angelou, Langston Hughes. They all motivated me to learn more about my history. My real history! They were not savages.

Regardless I still just wanted to see Africa. I wanted to learn about Africa! The allure of all the exotic places Tim buck tu, Egypt, and Ethiopia. People like the great Zulus, Sudanese, and Nigerians. I wanted to see the exotic animals, the lion, hippopotamus, giraffe, and elephant, just to see Africa itself! Just knowing today's world is indebted to the Black man for the contributions throughout our real history was enough. Knowing the forever plotting Europeans stole our Arts, Sciences, and History from Africa only made it worst. In my heart, I could tell Africa was a special place. No matter what the tv showed back then. I knew it was different! Back then, I never knew why but Africa was calling, and I felt it loud and clear!

THE MOTHERLAND

"The blood that unites us is thicker than the water that divided us."

Randall Robinson

Africa...Just saying the name feels special! Africa's name has history within itself. Africa is called by some "the Birthplace of humanity," Mainly due to the Great Cities of the pharaonic civilizations. These civilizations built the Great Pyramids being the largest and tallest buildings on Earth until modern times. Some say they were built during Khufu's reign (2590-67BC). His nephew Khafe built the Great Sphinx. Having his African features so boldly carved into it because he wanted everyone to see he was African. Africa has the oldest recorded history on this planet. With enslavement, the memory of many things about Africa had been lost in history. However, we remember Thebes, Kush, Memphis, Songhai, Kerma, Nekheb, and Moroe. We remember the Great Kings.

Africa is a vast place spanning 32,221,532 sq. miles. There are 1,287,914,329 people in Africa .Africa...The name itself gives me chills. The name Africa is to have been said to have come from many different sources. One source says that the Descendants of Abraham and Keturah themselves. These Descendants were known as Ophren. The Latin word is Apher. As time went on, the Romans, Asians, Arabs, and Greeks started to colonize the land calling it Africa. Strangely with time, most of Africa's states were colonized. Some places taken by unspeakable acts, and others out of war, religion, or deception. Deceived by the Dutch, French, Portuguese, Spaniards, even the Belgians, Germans, and British. Even Africans killed Africans by the thousands, all in the names of these savages.

Today there are only two places that are not colonized. Ethiopia and Liberia, the former an orthodox Christian community, the latter was established by African Americans settlers from the United States that were ex-slaves. Most African Americans don't even understand that Egypt is in Africa. Egypt, which means Black! It was one of the first great civilizations in the world. Egypt and the Greek version of the word Melanos means "Black!" The Egyptians called Africa "Khemi or Chem," meaning. (The land of the Blacks), or (Black land). From this word, we get alchemy and chemistry. I bet you already figured out why because the Blacks are very inventive people. The first so-called Egyptians were exclusively half African and half Asian. Their hostility to their mostly African others race was very social. The same effect would happen years later in the United States with slavery.

Egypt was then the northeastern region of ancient Ethiopia. After the cultural divide, the Africans held upper Egypt, south while the Asiatic Africans held lower Egypt and north. Chancellor Williams asked a question in his book (The Destruction of Black Civilization), asking, "How in view of civilizations' beginnings in the land of the Blacks, can one explain their role in the world history?" Having successfully degraded the Black Race throughout the world, the Catholics supported the degradation with their science and religion. "How may one explain that the same Black Race was the first of the builders, of the very civilization which the Caucasians themselves are heirs?" They tried scientifically to put the White man in Africa before Africans! Then that didn't work. They took Egypt out of Africa and said it was now the Middle East. Africans have always been inventive people, prosperous people!

Africans advanced in many areas before many different cultures and civilizations. Take for instance, the yearly flooding of the Nile River. This natural occurrence caused them to create the twelve months of the calendar as we know it today. They divided it into 12 months of 30 days simply to track the river's flow. Africans themselves invented writing; the African system of writing was very different from the Egyptian system. It was simpler and had vowels, whereas Egyptians had none. There were twenty-three characters letters in the African Alphabet, four vowel signs, seventeen consonants, and two-syllable signs.

Africa was the first in so my fields that it would take forever to name them all. Africans were the first to smelt iron. The Sumerians, specifically The Babylonians and Ethiopians, were the first to divide the decimal system. Africa itself is rich in cultural heritage, diversity, and resources. Africa is a vast place, and strangely this vastness creates a greater chance for innovation and greatness. Africa is the second-largest continent in the world in size. Africa also is the second largest in the world in population. Amazingly 14.7% of the world's population resides in Africa. Africa is larger than China, India, Mexico, the United States, and half of Europe combined. Still, in an ironic twist, Africa has the shortest coastline.

Positively because of the ridges and heights of their shores. Africa is the most centrally located continent in the world. Amazingly both Prime Meridians are zero degrees longitude and latitude. Some experts have even called Africa "The Center of the World."

Africa's vastness comes with greatness also. Greatness with its peoples and natural wonders. Here are a few. The largest country in Africa is Sudan; Sudan covers a total area of 967,940 sq. miles. That's 2.5 million kilometers. Sudan is as big as some continents! The island of Seychelles is the smallest country in Africa, spanning only 453 kilometers or 175 miles. Niger has the largest population in Africa, with 154.7 million people. Counting for 18% of the African population. South Africa has the highest GDP at 182 billion. Nigeria has at the point in (2016) the 20th largest economy on Earth. Five years ago, it surpassed South Africa as the largest economy in Africa. Nine of the earth's top 20 economies by economic growth are in Somalia, Africa. Equally showing our economic power. African Americans pose over 1.1 trillion in economic pushing power in America has the lowest GDP at 5.65.

With all this money floating around, believe it or not, Africa is a poor continent in the form of the wealth of its citizens. Strangely it is one of the wealthiest in forms of natural resources. So, I ask you. Why is Africa rich in natural resources, yet the people are so poor? Because of Structural Adjustment Programs (SAP) imposed on Africa by the Eternal Monetary Funds, World Banking. These organizations let invaders come to Africa, loan money, then charge an interest rate they know the lenders cannot pay back, thus keeping them in debt. This is why invaders from around the world have colonized Africa. There resources!

Still, before we get into that, let me inform you more of some of Africa's natural wonders. Africa's Nile River is the longest in the world. The Great Nile River spans 6,650 kilometers or 4,132 miles. Africa's island called Madagascar is the largest island in Africa and the fourth largest in the world. Africa has wonderful, majestic, and many one-of-a-kind places all over the continent. Africa is unlike any other place! For instance, Victoria Falls; this spectacle is listed as one of the seventh wonders of the world. Victoria Lake spans 2,683 sq. miles. The Great Sahara covers 91 miles in Africa. The highest point in Africa is Mount Kilimanjaro. Kilimanjaro is also one of the largest in the world. All these Great things are just a few fun facts about the most majestic place on Earth. Africa!

Let me remind you not just about the people. The animals in Africa are one of a kind also. Take the Great Wilder beast, or birds like the Greater Kuda, ostrich, Okapi, shoebill mauled Querenza, Grey Crowned Craine, and Galago, just to name a few. The tallest animal in the world comes from Africa. The great giraffe! Which today is sadly extinct in seven nations in Africa. The largest animal in the world also comes from Africa. The Great elephant! The most violent animal in Africa is the hippopotamus. The hippo kills more people in Africa than the crocodile and the king lion. Africa is a beautiful, mysterious, and wonderful place. Still, Africa is a dangerous place.

Africa is one of the most beautiful places on the planet. Yet also one of the most violent. Not just because of the wildlife. Africa is also deadly because of its people, which in my opinion, is normal when you are bread in an economical structure, where there is little chance to prevail. History has taught us all that poverty is the father of violence! Yet amazingly, six of the world's top ten countries with the lowest murder rates are in Africa. Question? If South Africa produces almost half of all the gold mined in the world. Why are they one of the most racially divided places in the world? Africa itself produces most of the world's Diamonds. So why a European Company like De beers control the Diamond market? Simple because that's billions of dollars. And with that kind of money comes deception, politics, and violence. This violence of greed has plagued Africa since the discovery of her Jewels many centuries ago. This is one of Africa's gifts and curses. Still, Africans have struggled, thrived, and survived through all of the politically motivated schemes.

AFRICAN PRIDE

"Africa whose badge of eternal honor was the Blackness of their skin. This color racism was deeply rooted, for it sprang from religion. They were children of the sun, blessed with Blackness by the sun. God himself and thus protected from his fiery rays, they were his children. Their very Blackness, therefore, was religious, a blessing an honor."

Chancellor Williams

What does it mean to be African? Your Blackness is your greatness! Yet, most Africans don't know this. The African Race is unlike any other on this planet. As an African, you pose more melanin in your skin than any other race. Melanin is a dark fluid processed by the pineal gland, which is larger in Africans than any other race. This gives us our skin tone, protects us from the sun, a historically thought by the Greeks to be why Africans could be so inventive, adaptive, and smart. Melanin is an intellectual chemical that scientifically was recently found to exist everywhere on this planet. Amazing! When concerning Africans from a physical standpoint, we get our unique swag and soul from, "Say it loud, I am Black and I am proud!" Still, with all this God-given greatness, it is still a gift and a curse. Africa's people themselves have been subject to numerous inhumane acts as well.

Take for instance, South Africa, I stated earlier that South Africa produces almost half of the Gold mined in the world! With this blessing come riches, wealth, and deception. South Africa's worst disenfranchisement of South Africa's Black population dates back to the colonial era in1948. Why is this year so important, you ask in a land-of-billions of horrific acts. In 1948 the National Government instituted a legal policy of "Apartness." Thus, creating apartheid, the world's most egregious racial divide. During apartheid, the Whites took all the land from the Blacks. Even after apartheid was so-called dismantled, they still took the land. The Whites planned to win! Then they bought, stole, and tricked the rest of them out of the good land that was left. Then they raised the prices of surrounding real estate, shopping, and food. This made it too expensive for the already poor Blacks to live there or go back. This was gentrification at its birth. In 2019, a South African woman named Wendy Goirana said, "I spent my whole life living in a shipping container, with extended family in Capetown. After the government said apartheid was over, we were happy. Then the Blacks took control and promised it would be better. But it hasn't! All I see now is corruption among the Black leaders, while the Whites still pull strings controlling all the money.

The world bank last year deemed South Africa the world's most unequal society! Estimating that the top 10% owned 70% of South Africa's assets.

In 2015 the split is still largely along racial lines. The bottom 60% being Black. How is that with all the gold, diamond, and coltan money floating around? Let me tell you how because the Europeans control the African resources. The people that got removed during apartheid were the bottom 60% are largely the descendants of Black and Asian slaves left from colonial mining. So, the Europeans don't care anyway. Today Blacks control only 7% of South Africa's wealth! Crazy huh.

What's more crazy is the fact that with all this Gold being mined. Half of South Africa's population lives on less than $5 a day. This is crazy! A typical job in South Africa pays around $10 a day. It takes $3 a day to travel to work by bus from the government-made slums. Gangs, which the government also controls, also controls this busing system, forcing some riders to even be on contract payments, with a $10 a week paycheck, $3 transportation fee, which leaves $7 a day if that. The government in South Africa never had good intentions for these people!

This is how it happened. In 1966 the Capetown Districts IX neighborhood, home to over 60,000 multi-racial (ex-slave children) peoples' land, was declared "Whites only" by the Apartheid Regime. They then came in and took the land! Then moved all the people to townships (slums), a desolate area 20 miles away from the city. Now, if you would pause for a second, this is where to me, the game gets tricky. Why? because this sounds a lot like American "Gentrification." When they demolished the inner cities housing, projects moved the residence outside the city to section eight. Then they develop the old areas rent/sale for higher prices. Like the half a million-dollar apartment they put on Bankhead in Atlanta. Then they police the section eight areas viciously while pushing in drugs and guns.

Thus, creating a different result, breeding a different type of person. This is in South Africa, yet I watched this happen in Atlanta and the USA.

South African sociologists attribute much of Capetown townships (slums), Gangsterism activity, poverty, drug abuse, and violence to the trauma of these forced relocations. Now I want you to ask yourself, with all these things, do the inner-city youth of America feel the effects of gentrification? Is this why we today have such a spike in gang culture, violence, and drug use today in America? In South Africa, the townships (slums) schools are horrific; 78% of the fourth graders can't read a simple sentence. I don't know about your life, but I know some kids in America Housing Projects that can't read either. In 2019 Axolile Notywla (general secretary of Social Justice Coalition) said, "even with a job, it's almost impossible to pull yourself out of this kind of poverty." She stated the word "impossible" that's crazy because some thrived through all the horrific incidents in Africa. Through all of this, Africa still remains one of the most beautiful places on this planet.

Throughout history, Africa has had bloodshed, unlike any other country. From the first Great wars in Egypt, Nigeria, Somalia, and Ethiopia to a host of religious battles. Africa still bears the scars from Asian, Arab, European invasions and their own civil wars. Africa still thrived! Strangely the people in Africa, well, most places are humble. Why? Mainly just like the Native American Indians, It was communal to be humble. These were religious and community-oriented people. When provoked, Africans can and have been highly violent to a level like any other race. For instance, the murderous Abu-Bakr or the treason of King Mambul, one of the first slave traders. This is one reason the Mozambique flag has an AK-47 embedded on the flag, which is the only one like it in the world. If that doesn't scream, don't bother us! I don't know what does. Africans are ruthless when it comes to holding grudges. The wars of Africa are many, yet some stand out larger than others. Take the second Congolese war that began in 1998 and lasted until 2006. This war was highly violent! Violent to a level that hadn't been seen in years. This war holds the second-largest death toll in history boldly at 4.5 million people! Standing only behind the infamous World War 2. Still, this war isn't shown on tv or talked about in magazines, exposing the funders or honoring the dead. Its place in history is still undeniable. This war involved eight African countries, spanning millions of miles, leaving rivers of blood.

Today Africa is a lot safer and united under one organization called (AU) African Union. The African Union is strong, yet; many say it is corrupted. The only country that is not involved in the AU is Morocco. The AU was established in 2001. The forming of this union stopped the Congolese war. This act showing the world and all Africans, together we can do anything. Today in Africa, we still have major problems, wars, killings, rape, and slavery. Wars like the ones in South Sudan, Defar, Buzmdi (DRC), the Democratic Republic of the Congo, and the religious war between Boko Haram and the Christians in Nigeria.

Today in Africa, we have problems like in Tarania. Tarania has the highest rate of Albinos in the world. Witch doctors openly hunt the Albinos in Tarania for the use of their organs. Crazy but true! These people are butchered for Rituals; these Rituals are believed to heal diseases. I know this stunning fact is hard to believe; hell, this is even movie-like, but all facts. These diseases they are attempting to heal are simple diseases. Which in most countries could be fixed with a trip to the doctor, yet they are all deadly in Africa! As Westerners, we think of Africa as an HIV/AIDS-infected place, yet most people don't know that most new HIV, AIDS cases, and crises are in European countries like Russia and Ukraine. Yet we don't see them on TV dying; why? Still more baffling is the fact that 50% of the world's malaria cases are in Africa. Three thousand children die a year from this disease alone, which could be fixed easily with Africa's untouched natural resources money. Still, it kills daily! Globally we have the technology and finances to fix these issues, but we don't! The fact that these people have little help fixing these issues is more disturbing than the problem to me.

In 2019 a host of communicable, curable diseases caused millions of deaths in Africa. How? Without help, that's how! Diseases like Lassa Fever, Dengue fever, cholera, and salmonella. These simple problems could be fixed by simply having medical supplies given out. It's horrible that in a land so rich, the people suffer so much. In Burundi, Africa, 39% of the children there are underweight. They also have a 41% child labor rate. These numbers are very disturbing yet changeable, very changeable. Only if we as humans do something simple and just care. Seychelles has a 92% literacy rate; let me say that again, "92% literacy rate. "Wow! In Chad, 13% and Niger 15% literacy rates. To me, this is crazy! This is very dangerous also. Crazy because in the information age, we still have people that are that illiterate or that unfortunate? Dangerous because, again, poverty breeds violence! In Africa, life is a misfortune to some. Why because there is less of everything, then there is also too much of everything. I once saw a tv show about helping give Africans internet service. This puzzled me because 74% of the 325.7 million people have the internet in the United States. That somewhere close to 290 million people. This number compared to Africa's Population of 1,287,914,329 people, only 453,329,534 of them have internet access. Astounding yet still way far under average. Today in Africa, the average person still has to walk 3.7 miles daily for clean water. Overstanding, I think Africans would prefer better water distribution than having better Google, Instagram, and Facebook services!

Some may say Africa is still far, far behind the rest of the world. In Africa, you still have unclothed villages or towns without sewer systems and electricity. For instance, the San people use the same tools found in African caves 40,000 years ago. The women in the Mursi tribe have been seen around the world! With their pierced lips. (The Mursi women insert clay plates as large as 5 inches in diameter). For instance, the Dogan people which are of Malian descent. This primitive tribe has plotted our solar system like no other, yet astrological scientists around the world still are baffled. How did they do this without a satellite or telescope?

There are 30 million people that visit Africa every year. With a staggering 10 million visiting Egypt alone. Why? let me tell you why, as one writer put it, "To visit Africa is to see God's greatest works!" Africa is special! We as Africans, are special! No matter how many invaders come, Africa will always be special! The people also. For some examples in other fields of expertise, here are a few. Take for instance, a tribe in Kenya called Kelenji. Kelenji produces most of the greatest, fastest, and award-winning long-distance runners in the world. Africa has too many excelling athletes to name, but I will name a few the Great Kipchage Keeino (cross country runner) or (global keeper) Lucus Radebe, (cricket legend Makanga Ntini, (long-distance runner) Haile Gebrselassie. Just to name a few. African's have always excelled in physical activities; just the physical build gives us a great advantage. Ironically, the invader's punishments forced your bodies to be made for stress and strain, which today is a gift and a curse. A curse because them breeding us for work led to some of the best NFL, NBA, MLB, and soccer players the world has ever seen. Africans invented the sport of Hockey hard to believe because it doesn't snow there. Let me tell you how. When the USA fought Britain and they lost, the British captured the slaves, where they sent them to Nova Scotia, where they played an ancient game, thus creating Hockey. Try the book (Black Ice) for more info. Today Africa's main sports are soccer and cricket; both were introduced during colonization. This colonization didn't just bring sports but a host of other new things, like Religion.

Africa was naturally among the first areas to which Christianity spread. Its located next door to Palestine. Moses was not only born in Africa, but he was also married to an African priestess. The Ten Commandments were already deeply embedded in the African Constitution ages before Moses went upon Mt. Sinai in Africa in 1491BC. The religious belief in sacrifice for the remission of sins was an African belief, a practice at least 2000 years before Abraham. Africa was the base for most religions; Efia, Vodoo, and Judaism were in Africa fifteen hundred years before Islam even came. White Egyptians control over the churches reflected the same policies that were followed centuries into our own day and times. No church-sponsored theological schools for the training of African clergy, thus preventing educational advancements. Deliberately preventing advancements and help. Abu-Fyha brought Christianity to Ethiopia with the Eastern Roman Empire. He was accompanying the Great Constantine. Amazingly still, Islam is the most widely practiced religion in Africa, an Arabic widely spoken. This is a strange fact. More people in Africa speak French than people in France. Wow! Let me explain how simple Africans vastness and population. The main reason, sadly, is because of French colonization and enslavement. For a second, imagine if all Africans spoke one African language. It would make us unstoppable! And we would have the greatest language in the world. Still, that is one of many amazing facts about Africa. I wanted to write this chapter close to the beginning of this book. So, you, the reader, could feel the strength, pride, and heritage of being African first! Then and only then, I feel we could succeed in changing who we are!

CHAPTER 3
ROYALTY

THE HISTORIANS

This next quote from the words of the Mali Griot named Kouyate spoke to me in volume about African history. It showed the authority and brilliance of the great men of Mali.

"We are vessels of speech; we are the depositories which harbors many secrets many centuries old. Without us, the names of the kings would vanish into oblivion. We are the memory of mankind by the spoken word. We bring alive the deeds and exploits of kings for the younger generation. History holds no mystery for us. We teach the vulgar just as much as we want to. I teach the kings of the ancestors so that the lives of the ancients might serve them as an example, for the world is old, but the future springs from the past."

It amazes me that Africans of the old times and today's times had their best and worst times displayed for all the world to see. Still, amazingly they thrived to become the most advanced civilization in history. This vast greatness has had its cost and repercussions. Still, they survived! Still, they thrived! All of the credit could be simply given to the persistence of the people of Africa. There are many morally correct leaders, warriors, kings, and queens. African's immensely bloody history has not changed the fact that Africans have had some of the planet's greatest leaders. Iconic men and women that came presented an ironically pasted. All of these people made their own undeniable marks in African history. Some good and some bad, don't get me wrong, some have been tyrants and committed horrible acts. My thoughts on some of those acts is that they were wrong. The deeper question to me in that is. Why didn't the world give more blame to the greedy outside influences? The Vones were pulling strings with political fronts. I will tell you why because the strings would lead to themselves. These groups have never meant Africa or its people any good tidings. My proof of this is simple; look at Africa's history. To invoke that much pain on people is simply not African culture but from history's past invasions, colonization, and tortures. This dog-eat-dog mentality and way of living was and still is very European. Chancellor Williams wrote, "We study our past for the express purpose of learning what made the race great in the past. What explains subsequent failures and weaknesses, and what in the light of that history we can do now if we have the will." This is what the study of history should mean to the African people in particular. Just for a second, let's just be honest with ourselves. Some of the world's greatest, spectacular, and miraculous civilizations ever to be erected on this planet were erected in Africa! Have you ever asked how or why? Take for instance, the Egyptian pyramids. By far one of the greatest spectacles of human existence on this planet. They were erected all with African, muscle, engineering, brainpower, and African know-how. The African construction methods, reasons, and skillset were phenomenal. Today with all the computers and technology and the brightest of scholars. We to this day, we still cannot figure out how these structures were constructed. Let me pose a question. With all of this know-how and technology today. Do we have the best scholars, scientists, and astrologers? It amazes me even now, thinking back on the past knowledge, dedication, and technology. They simply used the African way of life, training, and thinking. They simply felt if there was a problem, find a solution. Then they invented, they used their ingenuity, surroundings and prospered. Rodger F. Adams and W. Brown, both European writers, wrote, "There is evidence that in the days when Europeans were satisfied with rude stone tools, the Africans had invented the art of smelting iron to make tools." Archeological excavations have found the furnaces in which the iron ore was smelted. These are amazing facts and even more amazing technological advances in history for a race of people called feeble-minded and savages. Take for instance, the great university of Timbuktu. This historical marvel is where Africans happily taught their people and as African culture goes. They also taught all races, religions, and people from around the world. It's often been said that when the Europeans were garbed in animal skins, the Moors of Africa were wearing silk, linen, and cotton. That's definitely some great progress for savages if there ever was. Constance Irwin and James Baily said, "An inability to look through the window of ancient history with eyes united by ethnocentric eyes of this day. They and others have begun to provide a new script for the pre-Colombian drama of America. All the characters in the old world seem to have been given new lines. All except the Negro." They also wonder why? Maybe because with that truth, the history of European and pre-Colombian will be de mythic. Africans were not just smart people; ancient Africans were ridiculously proud people. Africans believed. "To empower one's people is to be worthy of the ground upon which you stand." Africans built their nations on hard work, dedication, family, prosperity, and loyalty first to the family. Africans progressed by putting that energy into the people and future generations. They taught the next generation whether they were on the battlefield, in the jungle, hunting, medically, or religiously. They taught them to provide for the family! The intuitive African communal structure was based on these things. Principals propelled them to excel. Just the African pride!

It was once said, "When the Hurricanes or the Hyksos invaded Egypt and took over. The Egyptians called this period in time as "The Great Humiliation." They felt ashamed, lost, and less than human.

"They felt the Whites were undeserving of power, and even passage in Africa. Comparatively speaking and simply put, "What our ancestors built is and forever will be beyond replication!" No other civilization has come close to what they built in Africa. No one has surpassed their prosperity or wealth even today. With that said, every Black man on this planet should feel immensely proud to be Black! Then make a conscious effort to do something to help promote that Blackness in a positive light. Then we as a people will grow together.

In the past, Africans didn't have the only great civilization on the planet. It is evident that in the past, they had some of the greatest leaders. Africa has had a host of great kings, queens, and generals. This is simply the reason for those great civilizations. Their past intertwined together in history. You cannot mention one without the other. Great kings like King Taharqa, Hannibal, Shaka Zulu, and Ramses. All great men that lead by example and yes, some by fear. For instance, the great Hannibal and Shaka Zulu both great leaders, yet violence was a necessity even (mandatory) in these times. Today even if we look at American history, sometimes it is an absolute essential ideology for a leader to be more feared than loved. A king back then had to be a warrior, leader, and scholar. These Kings still loved their people and fought hard, mostly to the death to protect Africa. At all cost! They fought not just to protect Africa but also the African way of life, community, and family. All this just to see the family, community, and country thrive. Was it worth it? Yes! Because they all thrived. Hannibal and Shaka Zulu were both great leaders, yet both will be known forever in history only for their violence, not for their compassion, Ideology, and intuitive nature. Shaka Zulu's reason for his violence was the liberation of Africans from slavery and colonization. If that's not compassion, I don't know what is. This brutality made him a great king and leader; nonetheless, it also solidified his place in history. Hannibal was one of the world's greatest concours yet; we hear more about Napoleon, alexander, etc. Why? In this chapter, I wanted to familiarize the reader with some of Africa's great kings and queens. This familiarization, I hope, will boil the blood inside of you and stir you into action if you are an African American male or female reader. I hope it will give you a greater sense of pride. I hope it sparks a fire showing you that an African Queen is the second most powerful thing on this planet. Following nothing other than her African king.

KINGS

"I am African first! I am Black first! I want what's good for me and my people first, and if my survival means your total destruction, then so be it!"

Sister Souljah

The African King's world of humiliation as a world figure began, in fact, with the coming of Christopher Columbus. Why? Because he was the first to initiate slavery in America. Thus, changing the history of the African male forever. The African King strongly believed that all people's failures should warn what to avoid and not as a justification for similar failures by another. History does not linger on the fact that the great sphinx was a portrait statue of the Black Pharaoh Khafre, also called (Cephreu). It doesn't linger on the fact that during their reign of Khufu (second Dynasty) (2550 –2567BC). The great pyramids were built. History doesn't mean specifically that the religious cults of Seth and Amon were all African. Why is it never stated or shown? That when the great city of Egypt was ever threatened by change or invasions by foreigners. It was always reunited or saved by the powerful Africans from the south. (examples) 2200 - 2050BC Menthtep I, 1770BC the Hyksos (Asians) invaded the north, 800 - 654BC. The Assyrians had made vassals of the northern kings; the Black southern kings reunified Egypt and held them at bay for nearly a century. It was at this point real Egyptian history began. Menes joined the two lands Ucizit with Nekkeb, which is the reason for the winged disk motif. We have all seen it on pictures, not knowing it was used as a political symbol of unification. Symbolizing the unification of the great two lands of Egypt. There are so many great Kings that it would take forever to speak on them all. Here are some of my favorite ones. I urge you to find your own; to do so, you only have to read our real history.

HANNIBAL

Hannibal will forever be one of the greatest military leaders in the world. His name undoubtedly would be on the top ten list of military strategists of all time. Hannibal was born in 247BC, around the decline of Carthage. Hannibal's father was a great warrior and fought alongside him in his first battle against the Romans. Early on, Hannibal showed a tact for battle and violence. He posed great strategy, cunning, and with time people Knew he would be great. Hannibal would grow in the army to command an 80,000-

man infantry, 12,000-man cavalry. Still, his greatest was the command of 40-100 deadly war elephants with all these accomplishments in arms. It was said that the elephants Hannibal had, were the best trained in the world. Hannibal concurred with all of Italy, Except the great city of Rome. Question? Why do you think Italians have such disdain for Black people to this day. Simple because of Hannibal! Hannibal was relentless, violent, yet dangerously smart. It was said that when he conquered Italy, he killed most of the men, and his army on purpose impregnated most of the women. Hannibal tried to break out of their race. Hence Italians unique features. Hannibal was recognized as being one of the most feared generals of his time. He was the first to march through the alps in wartime. The Romans put 90,000 men against him. The great Scipio led the army; still, Hannibal took his stand and prevailed. Hannibal was so detailed in his study of war that it was said that he would spend days studying the battlegrounds alone. Eventually, when battle time came, Hannibal would lead his military swordsmen and war elephants bravely. During battle, if needed, he would make adjustments from the battlefield and slaughter his enemy. Hannibal was ruthless. Still a man of honor and pride. Hannibal was a true African king. The greatest tactician! One of the greatest lessons that Hannibal taught his people and the world was that preparation wins wars! Even after Hannibal's defeat in battle, Hannibal still held his pride. Rather than surrender at the end to the Romans. The great King Hannibal killed himself thus, setting a tone for African Kings. No defeat, no surrender!

SHAKA ZULU

Shaka Zulu! Called by many "The King of The Zulu Kings." Shaka was born into power! Shaka's father was a great Zulu chieftain and leader. His father, Senorqakhara, was a stern and powerful man. He raised Shaka to be a soldier first, then a king. Shaka's mother's name was Nandi. She cared for Shaka dearly. She tried her best to change Shaka from his father's ways. She did this by installing love in Shaka and showing him how to care for his people first. Without this, she knew he would just be a killer instead of a thinker. When Shaka was twenty years old, his father died. The Zulu Kingdom was left to Shaka's older brother Sijuara. This inflamed Shaka! Shaka felt he should be king! He felt he was a better king than his brother. Shaka plotted and planned. Then one day, he ambushed his brother and killed him. In 1818 Shaka took over power of the Zulu's! Contrary to European history, Shaka was a great king. He was even a greater military leader and innovator.

Shaka was the first in Africa to separate his battalions into a skill set, training, and age. Shaka trained his men to use standardized weapons and special tactics. Shaka also invented to improve his army. Shaka Zulu Invented the assegai. (a short stabbing spear) Shaka taught his troops how to fight in a tight formation, and they used large shields to block enemy spears. Shaka had such a reputation that many of his enemies would run at the sound and sight of his army. Soon with time, dedication, and hard work. Shaka would turn a small tribe into a nation consisting of more than two million people! Shaka was also noted in history for his leadership; Shaka united all the tribes in South Africa to fight the European colonial rule. Shaka Zulu was a great leader, warrior, and king. Like most African kings had to be. His bravery, pride, and honor guided the Zulu's to greatness. The Zulus repaid him with a lifetime of respect. Since Shaka's rule, the Zulu tribe continued to use Shaka's innovations in battle. Thus, showing a sign of respect. Long after Shaka's death, his tactics and training provided the Zulus with respect. Shaka was a great king, and like most great African kings, Shaka learned young that power is taken, not given!

KING MANSA MUSA

King Mansa Musa, also known as Emperor Moses. King Musa was very, very important in the history of Africa and the rest of the world. Musa ruled the Malians from 1312 to 1337; the Kingdom flourished to extraordinary heights under his leadership. The Mali empire's name became a symbol of pride during his reign. King Musa expanded the Mali influence over Niger city, Goa, Timbuktu, and Dejenne. King Musa was a master businessman and economist. King Musa was estimated to have been worth more than 400 billion dollars. Let me say it again, 400 billion dollars! In the equivalence of today's money. This wealth would buy far more; King Musa was the richest man to ever walk the earth. King Musa Gained all of this by selling gold, Ivory, and agricultural products. All of these were the main commodities at the time. King Musa also had a vast army that kept the peace and constantly policed his trade routes. King Musa's army was also relentless in his pursuit of new territory. King Musa's army pushed the borders from Mali to the Atlantic coast of the west. They controlled land beyond Timbuktu and Goa to the east, from Taqhaza south to Mali, from north to the borders.

Taqhaza is where he placed his salt mines. Musa controlled land from Waquerin north to Mali.

Waquerin is where Musa kept his gold mines, which he had heavily guarded.

King Musa was a great Influencer at the University of Timbuktu, which was the world's first university and major learning center. Timbuktu was built not just by Blacks but it was built by the world. Timbuktu was a major spectacle! King Musa did a lot of great things, but his greatness in wealth was minor, to him providing his people with pride, knowledge, and prestige. Musa was a true African King!

QUEENS

"The real servant of the people must live among them, feel for them, and die for them."

Carter G. Woodson

Most historians don't relish on the fact that besides some of the greatest Kings on this planet. Africa has had some of the strongest women to ever have held the position of Queen! Besides the household names like Cleopatra and Sheba. You had warriors that were queens like Nzigaha, Cadice, or Asantewaa that fought harder than the men. Ramses II was the third pharaoh of the Egyptian empire. He controlled Cannon and Nubia all at the young age of 14. Ramses later marred one of the greatest Queens that has existed other than Cleopatra or Makeba. Ramses Queen was Nefertiti. A smart, intelligent, and kind queen. Who also helped her people tremendously. Thus, supporting the fact that to be a strong King, leader, man, you will need a strong woman. A real Queen beside you. Africa has had some of the strongest women to rule in the world. In fact, some ruled as lone queens, Before any other place in this world. Here are a few examples of Africa's strong queens.

QUEEN YA ASANTEWAA

Asantewaa ruled Kumasi, the central Capitol of Ashanti, a central part of Ghana. Asantewaa represented a supreme symbol of sovereignty and independence to the Ashanti people. At a meeting with invading Europeans, Asantewaa was so furious that she addressed the kings and chiefs. She stated that her ancestors were furious because an African king or chieftain would never let a White man or a foreigner talk to them as they did. She threatened that if the king's or chiefs didn't fight! She would gather the other queens, wives, and women, and they would take on all of the Europeans until all of them fell on the battlefield in death. This frustrated the kings and chiefs. (and stirred them into Action!). It motivated them to fight the Europeans. Asantewaa still leads the Ashanti in the battle when they fought.

Years later, she died fighting the British over the golden stool of the Ark, which her people had possession for centuries. The Ashanti believed the stool contained the souls of their ancestors. The stool was a symbol of respect and honor for the Ashanti people. They all would have fought to the death.

QUEEN NZINGA

Nzinga the amazon queen of Matomba the Angolan queen. Nzinga had a brother that was a king over a separate tribe. He was killed in battle over slave raids by the Portuguese. Nzinga vowed to fight the slavers with all of her power! She fought the Portuguese for nearly 30 years. She was pivotal in the struggle for her people's independence and strength. Those same qualities she brought to the people of Angola. She was even pivotal in religious battles as well. The Queen dropped her given European name "Ann" from her name. When she discovered that baptizing a Black into Christianity meant surrendering their soul and body not only to Christ but to the White man, She was one of the first Blacks to see that the Portuguese conquests, slave trade, and the church were all inseparably one and the same. Nzingha's second most pivotal move in Africa as she was the first African to Ali with a European country. She allied with the Dutch to fight the Portuguese slavers. A passage in (the destruction of the Black of civilization) by Chancellor Williams caught my attention. The passage was an exert from a Portuguese slavers' letter. It stated, "it's not true that all women and even children were likewise moved in chains. "This would have been unnecessary because we learned that those Black women are so loyal to their men that they would follow them into Hell. Capture their men and you did not have to capture them. Yet many of these same women would seek death directly by attacking our guards and us." During the time of Queen Nzignah's reign of terror on the Portuguese slavers. She was Harriet Tubman before her time. Instead of hiding from the slavers, she killed the slavers. It was said that she will forever be the greatest female military strategist to ever live. During her fight against the Portuguese, the Portuguese army commander, Bento Cardoso, tightened his noose on Angola and Nzinga tightened her onslaught on the forces protecting the land and her people. To the point where they had to come to talk to her and discuss a peace treaty in 1622. After years of battles and victories, Nzinga finely lost in battle, and instead of death, her captives knew she didn't fear. They Excelled her! This killed her a thousand times a day, and they knew it would. Why? Because they knew she loved her people!

MAKEBA QUEEN OF SHEBA

Makeba was one of the most influential Queens to rule her land of Sheba or modern-day Ethiopia. Makeba also ruled parts of Arabia. She was a great Queen and helped the people to grow and prosper. Makeba made Debanna her capitol. Makeba was a warrior and a queen but also a great seeker of knowledge and wisdom. Also known as the Queen of Sheba, Makeba was a wise queen and highly respected for her intellect alone. She was said to have taken a long and hard journey to Jerusalem to learn and just talk to the great King Solomon. It is stated that when Solomon met her, he fell in love with her. They even had a son. Their son Meneiki was also a great king. Makeba fought for her people and taught them to fight even harder. She is pivotal as a queen because she is mentioned in two of the largest read religious texts in the world! The Bible and the Quran.

CONCLUSION

Africa has had a lot of important kings and leaders. I could go on all day naming them and speaking about Important facts. Men of honor like Tharqa, which at 16, led an army against invading Assyrians in defense of Israel. This action leads him to a place in the Bible (Isaiah 37:9, 2 Kings 19; 9. People like the great saint Maurice Taure known as the Black Napoleon. Taure Conquered west Africa; he was the leader of the Roman Thyheban legion. Men like Bilal Al Ata Bashi, which was a companion of the prophet Muhammad. Bilal was a slave born in Mecca and was noted as the first Muezzin of Islam. Great Kings like Ramesses II, the husband of the great Nefertiti.

I wrote this chapter for a lot of reasons. The main reason was to remind the blind who read this book of not what they are and who they are. As Africans, you are the great descendants of honorable men and women. We as Africans in America, have forgotten this. We have forgotten the struggle before the slave trade, civil rights, and Jim Crow. The struggle that our people (you and I) ancestors had to overcome in Africa. This was civil rights even before the slave boats docked on the African coast. They had to fight! They had to fight in Africa just to stay in Africa. I wrote this chapter to re-ignite the thoughts of our power, our greatness, and our status as Kings and Queens. I hope these details about your ancestors stir you to voice your frustration and awaken your greatness! Just as it did with Nzigha and Shaka Zulu. I hope this chapter mentally prepares you for whatever battles you face in America as it did Makeba!

THE KINGS SET SAIL

"Through the process of historic, if we have forgotten that without us, they could never have become what they have made themselves appear to be. "

Mwalimu K. Bomani Baruti

For a long time, I why didn't Most historians speak about African Colonization. Ok, well, they do when it's concerning people coming into Africa. What they don't talk about is reverse African colonization. African colonizing different lands. Historians don't recognize Africans as seamen, period. Most historians have said, at the pre-Colombian era and before that. "Africans had no knowledge of the sea." Yet, the truth is Africans were navigating the sea centuries before the birth of Christ. Africans had the notion that the earth was round long before Europeans. They moved north thru the Atlantic to Ireland, capturing that part of the country in a very early period. Seamus Macmanus wrote of this in his book "The Story of the Irish race." Thus, showing that the Africans were great seamen long before most European seven tried to conquer the great Atlantic ocean. The court tradition of Mali and Cairo both have documentation of an African King of

Break the Chains

Mali setting out on the Atlantic in 1311. Strangely, the first pyramids, mummies, and trepanned skulls appear in America around the same time period. In this very period, a very dark-skinned figure appears in the valley of Mexico.

Some of these tribes even worshiped African travelers. The great Quetzalcatal and the Aztec god Tezcation were both believed to be African seaman. The Aztecs worshiped Tezcatlipoca simply because he was Black. I know, right! It's hard for many pre-Colombians, people, and historians to accept simply because of trans-Atlantic slavery's very negative propaganda, yet African Gods are not rare. Take the Mayan gods, the god of jewelers Neualipilli, or the god of Traveling Merchant's Exchange. Both were clearly Africans, who enter these civilizations strangely at the same time periods as the Mandigos set out on exploratory voyages. Honestly, when concerning race in African history, a good start would be to go to the ancient Greek and Roman historians. They simply told it as they saw it! The great ones like Pliny, Herodotus, Diodoes, Erashens, and along with the Bible.

Strangely all these historic calculations refute European interpretations made on African travel, especially by modern Caucasians. In the book by Harold Lawrence, "African Explorers in the new world "Hesitated," the works of Abu Zaid, Masud, Idris, Istalchri, and Albu Feda had trickled down to the University of Timbuktu. Scholars had come more recently in the time of Gaw and Mamodu, saying strange things. Like "the waters that washed the western end of Mali were not the end of the world at all, and the world had no end for it was built like a bottle gourd. His grout told him if you put your finger at any point on the gourd and tried to trace a line across it. He would come to the end of the line to the point where it first started."

This info stirred the African kings! Just the thought that there was more to conquer. This set the men to action. Look even at 1455 when the Portuguese sailors meet Gambians at sea. This fact seems to shock them into seeing Africans as real seaman. One of the most talked-about African kings tried to sail the great Atlantic centuries before European explorers. Was the great Mali King Abu Bakari the second grandson of a daughter of Sandiata. Abu Bakari was one of the greatest African kings yet restless. Restless because he wanted more from life than to be just the emperor of Mali. Which at the time was the greatest civilization on earth. Abu Bakari's empire was the largest in the world at this time. It is larger than even the Holy Roman empire. Larger than all the civilized states of Europe. The first coins to circulate in Europe since Roman - times were minded from his gold. He surrounded himself with people that were just as mentally restless for discovery. Scholars of Timbuktu who entertained the theory of a gourd-shaped world. He had dreams of this discovery; he loved to find out the truth. He finely decided to see for himself. He commissioned a voyage with many boats and many men. They left on this exploration, and for months Abu Bakari waited for their return. (some ended up all over the world) but still, none came back. This troubled Abu Bakari day in and day out. He would later again succumb to the call of discovery. He soon commissioned another fleet, this time with his own boat at the head of the fleet called Pempi. Then Abu Bakari one day gave all of his royalty and country to his brother and set sail. Just as his first fleet, he was never to return. Abu Bakari was a visionary before his time; what's sad about his legacy is that most people that don't search for real history will never know his greatness.

THE MOORS

Break the Chains

"A people without knowledge of their past histories origin and culture is like a tree without roots."

Marcus Garvey

Who were the Moors? The original moors were Black Africans, and as an amalgamation became widespread, only the barbers, Arabs, and Coloreds in Moroccan territories were called Moors. The darkest-skinned Africans became called Black Moors. Eventually, the Black was dropped, and they were just called Moors. These Moorish scholars traveled all around the world; with travel, they left African influence everywhere. For example, "castles!" Yes, castles, I know what you are thinking. England, yet the earliest model for a castle-built mote and all, was found in Nubia, Africa, in 18BC. This was before there was ever a known civilization in Europe. In 711, the Moors traveled to Europe to bring Europeans out of the dark ages. They spread religion, culture, architecture, and a host of other things that helped European civilization. The biggest was the medical field. How, why? Because up until 700, all medical books were written in Arabic. The Moors opened up trade routes throughout the world. Why do you think there are pyramids all over the world. Mexico, Japan, and America. They not only brought Islamic culture but other religions also. Ask yourself this. What is the largest race on the planet? African! Why? Because we were here first. We traveled this planet first! We were the originals! This was hidden, and the powers that be have gone to great lengths to hide these facts. "The burning of the Moorish documents and libraries in the square of Granada by Cardinal Ximemes in the late 15th century was done not just to be mean, but they knew those books held the truth of Africa and the worlds start of civilization."

The Moors ruled Spain for 700 years, teaching the Spaniards how to be civilized people. Giving them soap, silk, and linen. They single-handedly brought the Spaniards out of the savages into the light. "In 1599, descendants of Black governors of Ecuador chieftains visited Quito. These Africans were dressed in Spanish clothing yet had Indian ornaments on their noses and ears. They were the decedents of a group of 17 ship-wrecked Africans who soon gained political control over an entire providence in Ecuador. "This is one of many great things in African Americans history that was hidden from us. Hidden because if we knew who we are, then that would create a deeper hunger for us to be greater. A deeper knowledge for the truth in a negative co-dependent state our people's minds are existing in. They try and try to erase and annihilate our history because if they gave us that power, it would empower us 100%. They understand that knowing our history is your true power, and that means then you would break out of their system of racism."

Marcus Garvey once said, "Be proud of your race today, as our fathers were in the days of yore. We have a beautiful history, and we shall create another in the future that will astonish the world," with that said, I hope this enlightenment helps you to be a better you.

AFRICAN WORLD

"There is in this world no such force as a force of a man determined to rise."

W.E.B Dubois

When the African kings set sail. They had no idea that they would be putting in motion a set of events that would change the world. These kings had greatness in mind and the unwavering longing to find the truth. This stalked their thoughts. These questions plagued their dreams. Is the world flat? This question was never answered for most because the expeditioners never returned. Some even started new civilizations, and some went to old ones and became Gods and statesmen. In history, travel at this period was difficult; there was no GPS tracking, email, phone, or even a mailing system across the waters and land. When you set sail, you were instantly at the mercy of the sea, nature, and God. Still, we traveled; still, we conquered. Then they tried to hide our discoveries, a truth even harder.

In 1862, a colossal Granite head of Negroid feature was found in the Canton of Tuxtla. Near the place were the most ancient of pre-Columbian statues were found dated 800 to 7000BC. This discovery set off a firestorm of smokescreens. The scandal was concerning the discovery of the African statues of the Olmecs in Mexico. How? This had to be centuries before Columbus's arrival. Alexander Von Wuthenau stated in his book "The Act of Terracotta Pottery in Pre-Colombian South and Central America." "It's a contradiction to the most elementary logic and to all artistic experiences. An Indian could not depict the head of a Negro in a masterly way without missing a single facial characteristic unless he had actually seen such a person. "The type of people depicted must have lived in America. The Negro element is well proven by the large Olmec Stone Monuments and the Terracotta items and cannot be excluded from the Pre-Colombian history of America. One South African anthropologist MD W. Jeffreys stated that. "Negroes presence got to America before Columbus, whether by being a peddler, porter, a menial, mercenary (eternal slave). If so, then why would the people erect the largest monuments in honor of the workers? It's another thing to claim that Europeans, Northern Vikings or Southern Viracachas, brought "civilization" to the Americas before Columbus. This flies in the face of all the known cultural facts. The myths, rituals, and magic-religious system of Native America stand out in sharp contrast to those found anywhere in Europe. "Example" The agricultural system and calendar. A White God Quetzalcoatl is alleged to have introduced elements of both. Both are no relationship to ancient or medieval crops, science, and timekeeping among European people. In 62BC, the king of Suevians presented Quintus Metellus Celer with a gift of Indians, which were said to have been cast upon the shores of Germany. They were Africans!

Peter Marty, the first historian of America, reported that when he got to Dorian (Panama), he found Negroes in the providence. Professor of Anthropology in the Natural History Museum in Paris Alphonso De Quontre Fages in 1905 noted in the book. "Human Species" "The Black population has been found in America in very small numbers, and in isolated tribes in the midst of every different nations. Such as the Charaus of Brazil, The Black Caribess of Saint Vincent in the Gulf of Mexico, The Jammassi of Florida. He the African is not Enshrined, perhaps in an architectural monument, but his face broods over the Olmec's, his skeleton lies beside the ancient Mexican, a strain of his cultivated is found married to a wild American ancestor, his blood runs even in the veins of the Lacandons, the most secluded of the Mayan tribes."

A model of the Phoenician God Melkart in Rios Balsas, Mexico, was found with Hittile glyphs or obsidian disks or coins by Dr. Verrill in Utah. All these findings push toward Africans being in America thousands of years before Europeans. A mile outside the village of Treszapoles were discoveries that would change the way we view the Americas!

The Olmec heads were found and had a dating of 291BC. Startling enough, it was the earliest date then known for any American cultural finds. The Olmec head exposes the false, frail ground upon which the historical outlines of Pre-Colombian American history had so far been built. "stone reliefs of the Olmec culture of Monte Alban known as the Temple of the Danzantes (dancing figure). A series of Bas-relief figures on large stone slabs over 140 of these figures, most of them Negroidan Mongoroid mixer." This in itself is amazing, yet also in Morte Albain, where the Negroid dancing figures were engraved. Carving closely resembling an Egyptian Sphinx, and the Egyptian god Ra appears at the same location in its bird aspect.

"Ivan Van Sertina stated, "Extensive skeletal survey soften an Ancient Egyptian, both before and during, the dynasties show them to be roughly the same racial composition as the Blacks of a modern, Caribbean Islands with a predominantly Negroid base."

Oxford professor Anatomolgy Arthur Thompson, an Egyptologist of the same university, David Randell-Maciver, carried the most extensive surveys of Ancient Egyptian skeletal material ever made. They reported in 1905 that from the early predynastic period of the fifth dynasty, 24% of the males and 19.5% of females were pure Negro, between the six than the 18 dynasties. About 20% of the males and 5% of the females were pure Negro; an even larger percentage were intermediate with Negroid physical characteristics.

<u>Now I want to give you some examples on Africans around the world.</u>

SOUTH PACIFIC

Australia:

Australia was originally African land, thus revealing the origin of the original Australia, the Aborigines. In 1967 Aboriginal Australians were recently classified as humans. The Aboriginal people have had their own fights with racism. They had wars, internal and external, because of their Blackness. The original inhabitants of Tasmania were exterminated completely by the British. The Aboriginal people have been persecuted for their Blackness. They even tried to breed the melanin out of their own race. The movie "The Rabbit Fence" shows this. The Aboriginal people have also made some of the greatest inventions and gifts to humanity. The boomerang, obo, etc., all of these things helped them survive. Still today, they thrive and still are treated unjustly.

ASIA

Japan:

Alexander Frances Chamberlin wrote in the Journal Of Race Development in April 1914, "Even as far off as Japan; we can find traces of the Negro." Japan's army in the 8th century fought their rival, the Inivs vigorously. Japan's army was led by an African named Sakanouye Tomuramaro. Sakanouye would later become the first African shogun in Japanese history. Question? The Nambamn painting in 1500 is a painting of the Portuguese who first arrived in Japan. Tell me why in this painting, the Asians are dark-skinned, and the Portuguese are painted darker?

Malaysia:

The island of Malaysia is so secluded that over thousands of invaders, an African, Asian mixing races in the land remained the same. Take for instance, the Batteck tribe. This tribe has been secluded for years, and the people undoubtedly posses

African features. Just look!

Southern Thailand:

In Southern Thailand, there is a tribe called the Pidome People. The women of this tribe wear the same identical rings around the neck as the African tribes. Strangely not just this tribe resembles African features, culture, and habits, but a host of others like the Mani, Sekai, and Aman Islanders, Jarawaor the Jai pigmy direct historical result of the African Pigmys migration out of Africa, leaving some on the Island. The island of Fiji, Nequene all have African features. In Fiji, there was recently a scandal involving Ms. Fiji "Torika Waters," the natives' problem. She didn't look like them! she was light-toned, pointed nose, blond-haired instead of dark-toned, broad-nosed with curly hair. The people of Fiji were disgusted because they didn't look European. They were proud of their African features. This is how we should be in America.

Britain:

The Ivory Bangle lady found in Britain changed a lot of misconceptions about Britain. Usually, when Archaeologists found the bodies of Africans. They would write it off as a slave. With the Ivory Bangle lady, they couldn't. Why? Because she, unlike any slave found there was buried with gold, jewels, Ivory and showed a great sign of wealth and prestige. Even more baffling is that most of the greatest saints in Europe were Black, St. Calogero, St. Benident, St. Gregory, to name a few. How? Why? If we were savages!

Scotland:

After the Egyptians fought the Greeks, they took over an island naming it Scotland. After the Egyptian princess Scosha. The Greek and African mixed races produced the Scottish that we see today, dark-skinned, curly hair. Then the Arabs took all of Greek history when they conquered them. Today, we know most of Greek history because of the spread of Islam and the Arabs detailed journals.

Southern Mexico:

The Moors landed in Thresa, Porta, San Lorenza and traveled north, mixing with the Asians from the north in what we know today as America. Thus, creating a race of people with dual features. "The American Indians" The oldest South American tribe recorded in history was the Olmecs. The Olmecs were there before the Inca, Mayan, Aztec. And yes, they were very Africanoid in features. Discovered in 1837, the USA government quickly tried to get control over the discovery. Why? Because again, if there lies would be exposed! If people knew that, it would change their history. They placed Michal Coe as head of the Olmec excavation. The problem with Mr. Coe was he also worked directly for the CIA. He quickly shipped, hid, and lied about anything that proved the Olmecs were African. All except the statues, because they were too big, and they told a different story.

America:

One of the greatest misconceptions about Black Americans' mentality about Africans was that we came with the boat. This couldn't be further from the truth. The Moors were the first people to map the United States. America tells us that the pyramids built in Southern America (Collinsville, Illinois) or (Mississippi) were Indian. Well, how do they match exactly with African Pyramids in design and structure? Someone had to show them how, or they had to see it or did they just build it. Explaining why Western American Indians looked more African than Eastern American Indians.

<u>Hawaii:</u>

The founder of Hawaii was a Black man. King Kamehameha. It was stated that he would brag when he went to war with others. He would warn them that he would get his people from Africa to help him fight wars if needed. One of the most famous Hawaiians was the founder of modern-day surfing. His name was Dukek Ottangmoku. He was also Black! In the beginning, the Hawaiian government sent him to the United States to promote surfing for more tourism in Hawaii. When he traveled to different states, Duke had multiple roadblocks. Why? Because he looked Black!

All of these places have undeniable strong African Roots in history. What amazes most people is the fact that most of these places and people were not slave lands. I know how Jamaica, Barbados, the Bahamas, and most of the islands were created. Do you? Well, let me tell you. By slavery! That's why I wanted to focus on the non-slave places, showing that most of Africa's discoverers were kings and statesmen. Why? Because Africans brought with them culture, a new religion, and foods, even animals. I hope this chapter was full of useful information to the reader. Because as stated before. KNOWLEDGE IS POWER!

CHAPTER 4
INVADERS

THE DIVIDE

Africa was at once a peaceful place until her biggest secrets, was spilled all over the world! One expeditioner said in a letter to a friend about Africa, "They wear gold, diamonds, emeralds, and rubies like stones. So carelessly as if they lost one, they could quickly replace it." Africa was rich and when the world discovered this, the invaders came! The Asians, Greeks, Arabs, etc. They all came for riches! In the "Journal of African History," Sanders wrote that in 1783 Count Volney walked into Africa, and when he looked at these man-made mountains, and a strange guilt troubled him." He couldn't believe how great the slaves once were. This fact should trouble every African American male even today. "It was so natural to think of Blacks as hewers of wood and drawers of water. When did this curse begin? How we are astonished." "That when we reflect that to the race of Negroes at present are slaves, and the object of our contempt, we owe our arts and sciences." This troubled him because he saw us at present state a broken people, yet our history tells that we were once the greatest on this planet! We as American-born Africans, don't understand that we ruled at one point in time. Through acts of God or man, it all was dismantled. How did it all start? How did all this happen? Through colonization, migration, and invasion.

The first major colonization began simply, all because of nature. The drying up of the Sahara pushed Black Africans inward up from Central Sahara and Sudan toward the Nile Flood Plain. This northern migration of Black Africans into this Basin of the Nile made the land of Chem (Egypt).

Which essentially is an African colonization! The Blacks dominated the land from Africa's twenty-ninth parallel north to the tenth parallel south. This land was the old Ethiopian Empire. The Asian invaders constantly waged war against them, the African kings winning some and losing some. One of the biggest in 3400BC was won by the great African King Menes. The invaders took peace as a tactic, and as the Asian Europeans and Arabs begin to enter in increased numbers, thus pushing the Black Africans further from the Mediterranean. Pushing them to where we call today South Africa, thus making Egypt two lands. Exactly as Sudan is two lands today with the Arabs, and colored Arabs to the north, and the Africans in the south.

Alexander Moret wrote in "The Nile an Egyptians," Ethiopia means (burnt face). "Ethiopian Dynasty, a label given by the Egyptians historians manifested into the Black power period of Egypt is the Dynasty founded by the King Sofkush with his base at Napatain Nubia." In 751, Black Nubian troops of Kush brought Osorkon III, a Libyian King of upper Egypt, to his knees. They also crushed Tafnak, restoring Egypt to her former glory after invasions. They even renovated her temples, giving new life to the people. Also paying tribute to the Sun God, RA. Egyptians brought religion, food and gave their culture to the whole world. African Kings fought tirelessly to protect African and Egyptian culture. Kings like Piankly, Miamumnut, Shabaka, Tahorka, and King Tanutamon fought to unify Egypt and be great kings.

Alexander the great reached Egypt in 332BC on his world conquering rampage. But one of the greatest generals in the ancient world was also the empress of Ethiopia. This was the formidable Black Queen Candace! Legend has it that Alexander could not entertain the possibility of having his world fame and unbroken chain of victories. Scared by risking a defeat at last, by a woman. He halted his armies at the border of Ethiopia and did not invade. This remarkable woman, queen, and African is just one example of how they fought to keep Africa unified and Black. Puzzling to the Africans the steadiness of invasion, not understanding the Blacks, had what the world wanted most gold, diamond, ivory, copper, iron, ore, and themselves, as slaves! Ok, Ok, Now Let's not get too far ahead. This migration of Blacks inland also caused weakness between the once strong African ranks. The Divide was so strong that some even set sail. It's not strange that during the very period that a Negro-African donated the Serpent Crown of upper and lower Egypt, then mummies, Pyramids started to appear in America. Still, Europeans argue that they were brought as slaves. How when in most cases, they were found with wealth and their statues expertly done. Fact!

In no civilization has a slave been monumented greater than the Master. Africa's and African problems were just starting. The added accelerated depopulation of the Black man's countries resulted from soil, climate, mass enslavement, wars, and conquest. The ever-present inter-tribal conflicts, exhaustion from endless flights and migrations. Let's not forget the ever-present diseases. All this reduced the population, culture, and unity. This fueling the non-unifying of Africans slowly reduced them to ashes literally. This quote was in a book I once read on African colonization. And it summed up the vastness of invaders, colonization, and pain in Africa.

"What became of the Black people of summer?" The traveler asked the old man, for the ancient record shows that the people of summer were Black. What happened to them? And the old man sighed. They lost their history, so they died!"

After the Asian, Greek, and Roman occupation. The term Sudan came to represent the area not taken from Blacks. Soon European Imperialism replaced Arab imperialism. The Africans migrated out of fear! This fragmentation of official tribes led to grave isolation for some. This had two momentous consequences! The first was that the isolation of various groups led to over two thousand dialects and languages. The second was that the rise of these dialects led to the widening of the gulf between Blacks. When African chiefs and kings began to sell these slave-hungry Arabs slaves, they set in motion a chain of events to undermine the civilizations of the most advanced societies on the continent. Greed severed the traditional ties of brotherhood. The gradual movement of the invaders solidified the rest of their tribal isolation. Then the cross of Jesus Christ followed. What happened in the process of converting the Blacks to Islam and Christianity was the supreme triumph of the White world over Blacks. Conversion here meant far more than to a religion (More so in the case of Christianity.) This conversion meant a change in the White man's image to obey his ideals and value system. The real object of worship turned out to be neither Jesus nor His Father, but western man and western civilization. Millions of Africans became non-Africans. Africans who were neither Muslims nor Christian were classed as pagans. Therefore, they were required to dis vow their whole culture.

Practically all African religious institutions were regarded as backward or savage. The Blacks in their own race became nobodies. These strong psychological shackles still handicap us heavily today. The widespread segmentation and the disunity among the Africans made them easy to conquer and dominate. This is still relevant today. On learning these facts, I thought. Why didn't anyone save them? Why didn't they all band together? I have asked myself these questions a million times, and the truth be told, some tried to save us. Some tried to band together. You had some Moorish Travelers that traveled the world and warned Tribes of Invaders. Some listened and left going inland, so when the Europeans arrived at the villages, they were baren. The Invaders then just claimed the land as their own. In short, what we do deprecatingly call "tribalism" is, in fact, the necessarily cohesive and social mechanism for survival and defense against threats of survival. The tribe is the unit through which the race itself has survived during all of its migrating and scattered circumstances. Some African tribes saw Islam and Christianity as the White man's vehicle of conquest. The most outspoken was the Massi tribe. The Massi tribe told of a tribal prophecy that held, "When the first White man appeared in the land, the nation would die. "Painstakingly, this came to pass! Instead of using the old African system of brotherhood and unity to fight the invaders, they chose not to fight alone. Take for instance, the Lunar Empire. Instead of first attempting to conquer by anger and force. They would approach independent states and seek to demonstrate by oral history that all of them were merely segments of a common lineage (all brothers). So how did it happen that even now, in an advanced civilization, some of the most murderous and inhuman wars are fought by Blacks against Blacks? Without knowing that lineage was the most powerful and effective force for unity and stability.

In Africa, Blacks by contrast were not aggressive people. They only struck the oppressor in retaliation for prior wrongs done. Chancellor

Break the Chains

William said this "Testimony of history and perhaps this is why I have been puzzled by the declaration of Jesus Christ that the meek would inherit the earth." Did he mean the grave! That is a hell of a question! Considering that almost a hundred million people died and were enslaved. You had a host of races, religious groups, and cultures conquer Africa. The Ottoman Turks began their reign of terror in Sudan with the seizure of Sennar. This was done by Muhammad Ali, the greatest murderer of Blacks that ever set foot on the African Continent. This massacre of men, women, and children was on such a scale that even the White world protested.

Before the 16th century, most Africans on the continent had never seen a real White face. Some Africans were the boldest of unbelievers. They would venture out to rub the skin of the Whites to see if it were painted. Why? Because in most African rituals to ward off devils and evil, they would paint their faces White! Strange how now in today's western society, Black is considered evil and White is considered Godly. Chancellor Williams stated, "White was no longer the face of evil in the Black world; it had changed places with Black. Now Black was the badge of evil. All that was bad, even bad luck. To make a White man look evil, you had to dress him in Black. Even life's final tragedy death called for moving in Black! Happy events such as baptisms and weddings required the wearing of white. God himself, being White, had cursed the Blacks and made them the servants of man. For was he not made in the image of God? To worship God, In effect was to worship the White man."

This phycological play is another one of the slave's and oppressor's worst psychological tricks! Painstakingly this divide still haunts us in our travels. It haunts us in the way we treat the light-skinned Muslims,

Christian, Buddist, Efia. The dark-skinned, Morrocan, Sudanese. How does the east treat the west or Atlanta New Yorker differently? African is African, right!

SERVITUDE

"Philosophers have known for years that what trips up the slave is the desire to gain recognition from the master. We keep trying to persuade White people to recognize and acknowledge our worth as a people. We keep trying to impress the wrong person. When we need to impress ourselves."

Nathan & Julia Horne

What's a slave? A slave is a human being who has been reduced to being a possession with a fixed value. Some may say this word's meaning is un-Godly even the thought of owning someone pains righteous people right. Still, the Roman Catholic Church was one of the first to give permission to reduce Africans to slavery. With that knowledgeable facts, it can be deduced that they knew their acts were inhuman. Some may say it was even savagery. Then they might say, "well, there were Africans that owned slaves. "Oh, True! Some did, yet African slavery was never vital to Africa's survival. Africa never depended on a slave-based economy, and African slavery was never based on race. European slavery was unforgivable slavery! What made European slavery different were three main things. That scared a race forever!

1. The process of dehumanization:

    No other slave or race in this world was dehumanized. (prevented from being classed as human.)

2. Systematically barred from Knowledge:

The prevention from learning was classified as a federal crime. There is no other history of slavery where the slaves were not allowed to learn.

3. Worldly beneficial:

The entire world benefited from transatlantic slavery and colonization. No one helped out! On the contrary, they only added to the oppression. And they all got rich.

African servitude was different slaves were not sold. They would be indentured by wars or other means, but they still were able to be included with the captor's family; some would even marry the women. African slaves were never a commodity to Africans; this system is what the Europeans piggybacked off, which enabled transatlantic slavery to be far worse. Sadly, we still are a lower class of citizens, prevented from equal education, and the world is still benefiting from our present economic slavery and past slavery. The Portuguese arrived in 1444 at the mouth of the great Congo River in West Africa. Before 1434 the Portuguese believed the world was flat. All the way up until Gil Eanes dared to sail beyond the sea. The Portuguese were the first White Europeans to arrive in the west and central Africa. It didn't take long for them to adapt the Arab strategy of division by dividing the Blacks against themselves. This strategy was also used on the American Indians. That is why King Ma Mbull was one of the first slave sellers to Europeans. Sad but true! What I'm about to say now is more deeply disturbing than most of the things I've mentioned so far.

As of today, 04-30-21, there are three times as many people in forced servitude as were captured and sold during the 350 years of the Trans-Atlantic slave trade. This is crazy in 2021!

Astonishingly there have been actual slave auctions in Libya in the last decade. CNN aired a Libyan slave auction in 2017. In this footage, it showed What appeared to be African migrants being sold. Today currently, there is an average of twenty million people in debt bondage. A staggering fifteen million in forced marriage. The slave trade generates 150 billion dollars a year! Coming in second only to illegal drug smuggling. Question? If the system of slavery was fixed by the dismemberment of the Trans-Atlantic slave trade and the 15th amendment in the United States Constitution. How is it that slavery is worth more now today than at any point in history? How is that possible.

Throughout history, Whites have long ago defined themselves as a superior race. We can see this with their relations with the Asians, Spanish, and Native American Indian population. Therefore, the idea of subordinating an inferior race was already a part of the European mindset. Still, Caucasian's biggest fear is of the possibility of Blacks developing a sense of oneness, and unity of action is deep and centuries old. Many subtle schemes are still used to maintain divisiveness, and with much success, it has played out. Black hopelessness and internal strife have increased as external pressures and threats to our survival increased. The every man for himself philosophy quickly replaced the philosophy of external brotherhood. By that time, substantial numbers of Africans were in the midst of the system of forced servitude. This superior way of thinking eased the thought process and humanized backlash from the way slaves were being treated in their society. Meaning they didn't care how they treated other races. Europeans many fears of Africans and African Americans pre- and post-slavery. Since the Arabs left their mark on Africa with Islam, the Europeans have viewed the African as a conductor of Islamic culture. They also silently fear our history and structure. Many tactics were used to derail the Black man's path back to greatness. Sill as the great Mya Angelo said, "like dust still rise.

Throughout history, Blacks have been called a host of derogatory names. These names were Far from being just a deceptive term. They were meant to show others our worthlessness. They called us monkeys, niggers savages, animals, and super predators. Still, we excelled! They labeled us primitive, saying we were backward peoples "Primitive." I wonder did they realize that word also means "The first," "The beginners."

My question is to you, the reader. Why when primitive is spoken of in African past, we think of them as savages or backward? Blacks were called savages and primitive, in fact. Cool! Call them savages if that word pleases you. These were just the Blacks in retreat from slave hunters hiding in jungles and staying secluded. These were the Africans who had to choose between enslavement for life, all their descendants, or sulcation of freedom. They did not hesitate they chose freedom. At the cost of losing a civilization. A civilization which, in fact, they had already lost. The choice was To be slaves of Arabs, Europeans, or Americans simply meant becoming the foundation of their civilizations. Factually the United States would have failed if it were not for African slavery. If it wasn't for the kindness of the American Indians. Let's not be mistaken Europeans did not go to Africa to save the Africans. They went to Africa to save themselves! To find someone or something to stand on to profit from. This is the same pattern that the United States carries on today with Saudi Arabia, Iran, etc. Portugal was the first to go to Africa and gathered slaves in 1444. Some may say. Well, why didn't the Africans just fight back? Why? Because some tribes traded with the Europeans, and some didn't. The Europeans used their economics and pitted them against each other (pimping them). Using guns and Brandy. There is an old African Proverb that gives us a small thought of the Europeans Invasions.

"When fowl is eating your neighbor's corn, drive it away, or someday it will eat yours."

Ibn Batuta said, "The Sudanese women were so proud that when the White people took over their kingdom. They killed themselves rather than serve them."

People like Shaka Zulu, Queen Candice, Nzinga fought these people to death! They fought the most horrific part of our battle! They fought for African equality and Africa itself. Still, we don't give them their credit! So yes! Our ancestors courageously fought back against these barbarians, these destroyers of Africa! It's us! The descendants that have not to live up to the fight any whatsoever. Instead, we have aligned our cultural structure, religious beliefs, and blood with the enemy of our ancestors. This is a total surrender of our African culture. Over 50 million Africans were captured and enslaved! Staggering huh! But what about the other 50 million that died fighting the slavers and invaders in Africa.

Fifty million slaves are over the 1870 US population, which was 38 million people. Imagine the entire United States in 1870 captured and enslaved. Then beat, raped, and sold around the world like animals in a cage. There were at least two million slaves taken to the West Indies, eight million were sent to Brazil. Two hundred thousand were imported to Mexico. All before the beginning of the 19th century. The slave trade generated millions very fast! In 1820 Alabama had forty-one thousand 879 slaves. By 1860

Break the Chains

they had four hundred thirty-five thousand. Mississippi had thirty-two thousand eight hundred and fourteen. By 1860 they had four hundred and thirty-six thousand six hundred and thirty-one slaves. Initially, the sugar trade boosted the slave trade in the 16th century. The sugar trade fueled the slave trade until the American Cotton Trade came. These are the reasons Africans ended up in Brazil, Barbados, Jamaica, Bahamas other islands.

The Cotton Trade came in the southern United States, thus igniting a greater fire. Over half of all immigrants coming into the United States between 1500 and 1800 were African. 97% of them sent here against their will. Most of these slaves came from larger regions in West Africa below the Sahara Desert known as Guiana, Angola, An Gambia. Today in 2021, there are slaves, poverty, and death in Africa! The French an American military are all over Africa, pillaging her resources and starting profitable wars. Strangely the biggest Black market for guns in the world is in Africa. Why when most are not made there? For centuries Africa's natural resources have been a major factor in all these issues. Africa's gold, diamond, etc. Foreigners have come and taken what they wanted either by force, killing thousands, millions, by deception. Sending them into poverty or systematically moving them. Painstakingly were not talking about past Africa, but today's Africa. Today in Africa, these monstrosities still exist. This is still happening! These outbreaks of diseases, mass starvation, and water shortages are not all-natural. These things are being done intentionally. These things are being done in plain sight of the worlds watchful eye. Still, nothing is being done! Still, we as Africans are blindfolded. Why? Because of Greed and Money!

Tragically in 2018, a van packed with illegal African workers died in a car crash. There were sixteen men from Morocco, Senegal, Nigeria. Someone's father, brother, and son. All were illegal slave workers! In 2018 that is crazy! Most illegal migrants workers in this system are from sub-Saharan Africa. Your mothers, fathers, culture bloodline still suffer. Abu Bakr soy Mahoro said, "The rope of desperation has replaced their iron chains."

Desperation is because, according to a DOB Gates Foundation Report, that said, "by 2050, 40% of the world's poorest people will be living in the DRC (Democratic Republic of the Congo) in Nigeria. This rapid descent to starvation, disease, an early death generates an exodus of youth trying by any means to save themselves or their family. Reminds me of post Exodus, when the Europeans captured slaves stealing land, and more. Still today, this Exodus also creates a monster that is fed off their struggle. Energizing the situation that is powered by the current rules and laws that only tighten the grip on these already beaten people. Know if you are so naive to believe there are not laws, rules, etc., set in place to keep Africans of any country docile and oppressed. Then you need to read this book twice, Hell three times until you see it clearly.

I want you to ask yourself, is this all planned for real? Simply because it's too hard in Africa to find work, food, water, and health care. Ask your self would you risk your life being abducted and enslaved for something fake. These people try to escape illegally, Then when captured. They were not put in cages like the Mexicans by the United States in 2019. They are most likely sold. The men to farmhouses to work in modern-day servitude/slavery on work camps and plantations. The women were forced into prostitution! In 2016 a report found that seven out of every ten migrants crossing from North Africa to Europe. Had experienced exploitation, forced labor, illegal detention, and sexual violence. Some African officials even say humans are being sold because the Embassy won't give African Visas. It's obvious how to fix the problem. All we have to do is give the people in Libya, DRC, South Africa, and Nigeria a reason to stay home. Give them a chance to prosper! Then they wouldn't risk their lives to go to Europe.

Just as I stated earlier, In the past, Europeans and Americans have worked hard to class all of African Society as primitive, savage, and uncivilized. This was done mostly to justify the enslavement and treatment of the African People. Most African tribes were civilized people, loving with a well-developed economic and political system Before the Europeans arrived. This kindness and naivety are what led a lot of them to be deceived. For instance, the residence of Upper Guiana has always had substantial commercial contacts with the Mediterranean world. They traded Ivory, Gold, Silver, Diamonds, and Slaves. Yes, slaves! Ghana's religion makes up mostly Islamic due to most Ghanaian as merchants travel. Even more impressive is their will to survive after the collapse of the Ancient Kingdom of Ghana around AB 11,000. They again created an even larger empire. The kingdom of Mali! Mali then survived the 15th century, then the invaders came, and the great university of Timbuktu became faded. It no longer was the world's center for education. Sadly, they then still were captured and enslaved. Have you ever heard of the Mamelukes? The Mameluke was White and yes, slaves. In 1250AD, they lead a murderous onslaught against the Turks and Arabs. Thus, forever ended the enslavement of Whites in Africa. All they did was fight back together!

Historically, Johann F. Blumeback, 1752-1840, a German was the first to divide humanity based on skin color. American slavery became legal in the early 18th century. This was when the colonials began to pass slave codes, thus granting White masters almost absolute authority over the slaves. Only one factor determined if a person was subject to the slave codes when the laws were passed. "Color!" Unlike in the Spanish Colonial Societies, where the people of mixed races were granted a different or higher status than pure Africans. English Americans recognized no such distinction. They felt any African Ancestry was enough to classify a person as Black! "From the pride of racial worth an identity, the Black man's mind generally operates favorably toward his White enemies and negatively toward himself and his kind." The Willie Lynch Syndrome!

In 2019, the Global Slavery Index found that G-20 countries import 35.4 billion dollars' worth of products produced by modern-day slaves in Italy. What! Right now, in 2019 is a push to produce "slavery-free" foods. This is crazy! Absolutely absurd to me also. Why? Because in today's time, we have multi-billionaire Africans Spending millions on bullshit! These same Black billionaires fight causes like no GMO foods or fur protection. Bullshit! This is what they fight for when their people getting beaten, enslaved and raped. Not just any People, your People. Black People!

We as Africans have forgotten about the ones in Africa, as well as they have forgotten about us! Has anyone ever asked themselves how the Trans-slave trade affected the Africans left behind? I will tell you; the slave trade made Africans uncomfortable and deadly isolated with themselves. They lived in fear of each other because they might come to enslave your tribe. This mentality is the reason in Africa the people are separated now. Do you not know that when Napoleon marched into Egypt! The scientist of that expedition was equally astonished and impressed by what they saw. They concluded as the Greeks had done thousands of years before their arrival. That Egyptian civilization owed its Inspiration to a Black Race! Ivan Van Sertima said, "Every new archeological find seems to be pushing the agriculture breakthrough in Africa further and further back in time, and their influence on ancient Egypt should not be underestimated." Blacks had long ago been great kings, queens, and statesmen. I pointed this out because we have to realize we were great.

Ivan also stated that "While Egypt gave nothing to Black Africa, Black Africa contributed the bolt bottle gourd, the watermelon, the tamarind, cultivated cotton and themselves as slaves!"

We not only helped America to prosper, but as I said earlier, African enslavement was a worldly benefit. We have to break the barriers of slavery's wall and reunite to become one. I know you are probably thinking, wow, all this is going on in the world and in Italy? How? An nobody noticed it! Let me explain how. They did it using Cap-oc-al-oto. This Italian word means a system of press labor. This system enables farmers to outsource their labor to middlemen for a set fee (sharecropping). When they do this, they avoid payroll taxes, work safety requirements, and minimum wage payments. I know what you are thinking, and Yes! This is very illegal. And Yes, this is very widespread. This system is mainly dominated by Italian organized crime. Wow! It's ironic to me that in a world where African American males idolize those Italian mobsters. They are balling off your ancestors' offspring and bloodline!

A 2018 report by the Italian Union estimated that in Italy, 132,000 plus workers are illegal and are currently being sold and exploited by Caporalto.

These African are mostly from Sub-Saharan Africa. The Italian internal minister Matteo Saleini, also the head of the far-right anti-migrant league, said this. "The Mafia's role in the Italian labor practice is detrimental to their finances to stop Caporalto is stopping Italian organized crime!" Julie okah-Donli The (Director of Nigeria's National Agency for the protection of trafficking) Witnessed this herself in 2006. She saw people living in slave-like conditions, being worked like slaves. This is crazy! When we live in a so-called Humanitarian, politically correct world.

There was a story I once read about a 12-year-old girl. She said she and other captured girls were locked in a dark basement for days. No food, water, or bathroom. They got nothing until they submitted their virginity. These innocent African princes defiled by these savages breaks my heart and it should break yours also. She said they were starved for days! Then she said that when she finally broke down and submitted. She only got a bottle of water after they raped her. This is horrific! In a world where African Americans live so carefree, This is horrific because I have daughters, aunts, cousins, and a mother! How could any African American with the means to help not! This is horrific. What if this was your daughter, aunt. What would you do to save them? I ask Jay Z, what if this was blue? I ask Kanye West, what if this was north? I ask Steve Harvey, what if this was Lori? I ask all you so-called rich African Americans, what if this was your child? How far would you go to save them or prevent this from happening to them? Well, it is someone's family, someone's child. Remember the African proverb that said, When you see the crow eating your neighbor's corn, soon he will eat yours.

In the Italian city of Asti there is an organization called P.I.A.M

(Progetto Inlegazione accoglienza Migranti). Its Founder Princess Inyang Okokon was trafficked, yet she escaped. Now she helps others to escape this life of pain. As of today, there are an estimated 700-1000 girls that need help in Asti Alone. What to me is disturbing is the fact that the shelter there only has space for two hundred and fifty women. Painstakingly some women stay on the waiting list for months. During this time, some get recaptured, resold, incarcerated, or killed. Know I want you to ask the females this. How in the world where we have Black American, or African American Female Billionaires, millionaires, and millions of African empowered women all over this planet. That these women do not receive better aid? Still, in Hollywood, a sexual harassment case where an entitled producer (Harvey Weinstein) asked an entitled gold digger to rub his feet. Gets more airtime than this situation on the news. It's crazy! That they try us like this in our faces! This smokescreen world we live in is horrific. Still, some want to keep trusting their process and plan their lives, moves, and future according to their rules, values, and religions. (In my best Italian mobster voice) Fuck Outta Here!!

CHAPTER 5

SLAVEBOATS DOCKING

DEPORTATION

The Portuguese arrived in Africa in 1444 in ILe de Gore`e of the coast of Senegal. In 1462 they created the city Capo Verde present-day Santiago. They then enslaved the local Waloff tribe, which taught the foreigners how to grown sugar cane, cotton, and weave. Around 1510 they started to export Africans as slaves to the Caribbean island for their sugar cane plantation. With time everyone wanted in on the trade of African slave labor. In 1562 England joined in, followed by Holland (the Dutch) in 1626, French in 1640, Denmark (Swedish) in 1650. In Africa, it is said that with the first slaves, deportation and shackling, the Maafa began. This Swahili word means paraphrased. "Black oppression." Apart from being captive, One of the worst parts about African slavery's time was the passage from Africa. This trip had to be horrific! There were a staggering 5,400 documented voyages in 300 years. They were distributing our ancestors like an economical product. This trip even for the most seasoned warrior. Had to be a living death! American history tells us that Christopher Columbus brought the first Africans that came to America. Factually we all know that is untrue. Africans were here before. The African descent in history only began with the coming of Columbus.

The African to America slave trade started in the 15th century historically. It lasted for years unchecked! Africa lost an estimated one hundred or more million people. Over 20 million were documented and shipped out of Africa. Just one recorded file of the Trans-Atlantic database estimated in years 1528-1866. Twelve point five million Africans were

Break the Chains

shipped! Staggeringly an estimated ten point seven million men, women, and children survived. Most then were shipped to America and the Caribbean. That's around 15-30 percent. So, for every one hundred Africans, forty of them died on the trip of enslavement. Have you ever seen how chickens are packed tightly on an 18-wheeler before the slaughter? Know if you could take a second and imagine how it felt to be shipped like those chicken for months! That's crazy, they treated our ancestors like cattle or livestock.

There were an estimated two hundred and fifty to three hundred slaves per boat. The living conditions on these boats were horrible. They were chained in a space five feet three inches and four feet wide like cattle! The slaves were barely fed. If they did eat it was one of three things corn, yams, or rice. The slavers painstakingly brought or, better yet, kidnapped little girls between the ages of six and thirteen to be used as sex slaves. Why? Because they normally couldn't get pregnant or had minstrel cycles. How sick of a person who lives like that! When many African leaders found out what was going on in the USA, they were outraged. Madomn Tinubu, a leader in now Nigeria, was the first to sound the alarm about African treatment in America and Great Brittan. She then returned to fight harder against the oppressors.

One of the bravest Black leaders, Mr. Marcus Garvey, once said, "What do I care about death in the cause of the redemption of Africa. I would die anywhere in the cause of liberty. A real man dies but once! A coward dies a thousand times before his real death. So, we want you to realize that life is not worth its salt, except you can live it for some purpose."

Over five million estimated slaves died on this bloody passage. The survivors were most likely shipped throughout the Caribbean to fill sugar plantations. There is a low estimated 500,000 that landed in America. This is why today Brazil has the largest African population in the world.

African Americans' enslavement was unlike any race on this planet! The Trans-Atlantic slave routes altered two things in nature itself. How? It altered the migratory pattern of sharks. You're thinking sharks. Yes, sharks! They were feeding on the dead bodies of the slaves! Some captives were jumping intentionally, knowing that death was better than what was coming ahead. This is still the same migratory pattern that they travel to this day! The Trans-Atlantic slave routes altered a lot of things in history. The most impactful thing it altered in nature was the mindset, prestige, and thought process of Africans worldwide then and even today!

SLAVERY

"Nothing the future brings can defeat a people who have come through hundreds of years of humiliation and privation with heads held high and eyes clear and straight."

Paul Robinson

In 1619 the first Negroes to arrive as slaves on record arrived in the United States. Their names were Anthony and Isabella. In 1624, the first African child on record was born into slavery. His name was William Tucker. Without thinking through historicide, we have forgotten that America could never have become what America is today without us. African slaves cleared fields, forestry swamps, built roads, bridges, buildings, and dug canals. They even built the great White House. They created a base for wealth or the Europeans future generations. Robin Black

Burn wrote in his book "Them king of the new world slavery in 1996" "That while race was a factor in making the enslavement of Africans easier for Whites to justify to themselves. The real reason for the emergence of slavery was hardened economic decisions by ambitious entrepreneurs. Who realized very early that slave labor was more profitable than the current labor system. Slavery boosted the economy in the south and east coast. They didn't care how they treated the slaves, yet they profited from the cotton and its products. When the slaves arrived in America, it was for their benefit. At its center, slavery was a major topic at times. People debated whether slavery was the result of White racism or was racism a result of slavery.

In 1950, Oscar and Mary Houldin argued in a published article, "That what separated slavery from other forms of servitude, is that it was restricted to people of African descent that it was passed from one generation to the next, to increase the available labor force. The distinction between the conditions of White workers and the contributions of Blacks was therefore based on legal and economic motives, not racism. Winthrop Joran, who later challenged the Houldin thesis, argued in "White over Black 1968" that Europeans had long viewed people of color and Black Africans in particular as inferior beings, appropriate for serving Whites. Those attitudes migrated with White Europeans to this new world while racism shaped the treatment of Africans in America."

In 1850 Joshua Ward from South Carolina owned more than a thousand slaves. This made him the largest slave owners in the United States. Second only to Stephen Duncan from Mississippi, during these times, African slaves were preferred over Indians. Why? Because the Africans were millions of miles away from home. Europeans learned through trial and error that Indian slaves were trouble. When enslaved, the Indians would flee to their brothers and sisters; then, they would come back armed, fighting to death. Still, the Europeans captured Indians and enslaved them, sending them to Great Brittan, Barbados, etc. The Indian slave trade is what saved and started the Carolinas. In the 1600s, European explores would seize Indians for sale or training as interpreters and guides. In 1611 English slave Redward Harlow went on a captive-taking spree from Monhegan Island in Maine south to cape cod. Again, we as Blacks have forgotten that the land we now stand on was the possession of indigenous people. The Indians! Who are now disproportionately incarcerated on reservations right now? History tells us that Black Americans and Indians have mixed since Columbus arrived in America.

African and Native Americans have a lot of similar cultural, religious, and tribal similarities. So, the Indians felt sadness seeing the Blacks in bondage. When they realized the Whites were putting them in bondage, they helped the Blacks. The first full-scale battle between Native Americans and British colonists was Jamestown in 1623.

James H. Johnstone wrote, "The Indians murdered every White man but saved the Negroes."

Why? This is the question many have asked themselves. It's simple, just as in African tribes, most Indian tribes were peaceful, understanding people until provoked. Many slaves escaped the oppressors and fled to Indian lands, becoming a part of those Indian tribes. When slaves from Georgia ran away to the Florida swamps to the Indians. The Indians would hide the slaves when the slave masters would come looking for them. That was historic! I once read in a book that Whites argued with Indians about slaves and private property rights in owning African Slaves. They insisted to the Indians that the Africans were inferior. The Indians always shrugged their shoulders, saying, "NO!" As time went on, the images of the Native Americans promoted in books and newspapers became insanely negative. This was done to persuade the people to believe that eliminating the savages was less of a moral problem and more for safety. This again justified the Indian's extermination. Strangely this negative propaganda trick was done years later with African slaves. It pains me to think about the Trail of Tears or the many Native American massacres.

The African arriving in America simultaneously were treated even worst. Over 40% of the Africans arriving in the New World landed in Charleston, South Carolina. During this time, Charleston was considered the center of the United States slave trade. African slavery Skyrocketed Charleston's economy into prosperity and wealth, the same wealth that a lot of Charleston's White population still live off today. Nearly a quarter-million Africans brought to the United States were from Angola Africa, which is crazy! Why? Because Angola is also the name of one of Louisiana's biggest plantations. Ironically now it serves as a prison still housing African Americans! The second-largest group of African slaves was from Senegambia.

The slaves arriving at these ports would be washed, clothed, and rubbed with palm oil to disguise sores and wounds. Then they would be sold at auctions to planters or wholesalers. This was when the bloodlines were broken, the families broken, and sold to different plantations. At these auctions, the going price for an African slave was 3,978 in the north; in the

South, it was $2,040. The United States' average price for a slave in 1860 was $1800. Next, the slaves would arrive at the plantations. On arrival, the women would be separated by age or the one the owners wanted to work or rape. The men would be sent to cabins to start the seasoning faze (breaking in). During this time, many slaves committed suicide or fled. The seasoning fazes normally lasted three years. This is when most slaves would run north, thus separating the bloodline even more. Imagine your father, mother, sister, and brother being snatched from your arms. Taken in a place new to everyone around you. Imagine your young teenage sister's fears when these White men take her with lust in their eyes. If not already scarred by multiple rapes mentally broken by the other horrors she has witnessed. This day still would be horrific! These pivotal points in slavery were when the mental chains were placed. This was when slaves were broken like horses, beaten, and tortured. This was when the effects of the chains did its worst damages. This point in history is one of the most pivotal points in this book. During these times, the great stories you have heard about the Master finding the biggest male in the groups and torturing one on purposely in front of the group brutally, in the presence of the women and children. This was when the "Willie Lynch" mentality was installed. This process would install fear in the women. This fear would be relayed to the sons and daughters. This created a mental chain of fear of the White man. A chain of inferior thinking, an inferior mental chain that we still suffer from even worst today! This chain is what created gangs, hoods, and a deep hatred of our own Blackness! This chain is what made the world think of us as inferior people. This chain placing is what served our culture, bloodline, and history.

Slavery was legal in 13 colonies at the time of the Declaration of

Break the Chains

Independence in 1776. slavery lasted until 1865 on record. Economically it was replaced. Sharecropping and peonage (convict leasing). Then ultimately, the prison system, but let's not get that far ahead. During this time, when slavery was set in place as an economic system, some slaves even bought their freedom by the process of "manumission" (The voluntary Emancipation of a slave by owner). This process got to be rare as the 1800 progressed. Almost all African American slaves brought to the United States were Christian. By the early 18th century, some converted voluntarily, and some after coercion from the bullwhip. The traditional African religion of respecting an Almighty God and a hierarchy of lesser deities was later taken over by the Christian in the form of Patron Saints and higher deities who rank next to God himself. Protestant missionary slave masters expected these slaves to worship under the supervision of White ministers. This prompted slaves throughout the south to develop their own version of Christianity. They did this by incorporating such practices as Voodoo or other polytheistic religious traditions from Africa. The new African religious practices were more emotional than its White counterparts and reflected their African influences of customs and practices. Slave prayers routinely involved fever and chanting, spontaneous examinations from the congregation, drums, and ecstatic conversation experiences. That is why you can easily see the difference when attending a White church or a Black church in the United States.

In Edmond Morgan's book "American Slavery American Freedom 1975," he argued that "The Southern labor system was at first relatively flexible, and later grew more rigid," he claimed. "This system did not intend to create a system of permanent bondage for Blacks! He stated because tobacco prices grew, it created a high demand for cheap labor. In short White landowners felt very uneasy about the dependence on a large group of White workers, slavery, therefore, was less a result of racism and more of a desire for Whites to find are liable and stable labor force." It's strange that as time went on, Blacks were stereotyped as lazy. That's absolutely absurd when Europeans main excuse, other than race for our enslavement, is because they were too lazy! The current stereotypes of Blacks as extra aggressive and unruly sexual predators can be traced to this point in our history also. We all know the propaganda of White men fearing an angry mass of Black men rising up to attack them or rape their women. Again, it was the opposite way, and they knew it. They were the aggressors, the rapist, the super predators!

In the 1630s, the first legal rules changed for Africans across the world. It started on the small English-ruled island of Barbados when the governor announced, "All Negroes, and Indians should serve for life unless a contract was made." Once again, our native American brothers suffered with us. Staggeringly in less than half a century, indigenous Americans lost ninety million acres of land, two-thirds of what they owned. Over ninety thousand people become landless, homeless in the country of these ancestors. All deposited in mostly Arkansas and Oklahoma land the White considered uninhabitable. "Powerlessness breads a race of beggars" (Charles Hamilton). I will always think of this quote when I think of their plight.

Again, the Europeans treated the Indians horribly, killing them with diseases, Gattlin Guns, and other inhuman tactics. Still, they raped their women or kidnapped their beautiful daughters. All behind the banner that they were savages and unholy. Which again was the total opposite! The

New Founders of America were the savages, the killers, the unholy men that God himself despised. They enslaved both races and profiled off them. The racist Charles Darwin wrote, "It's not the strongest of species that survives nor the most intelligent, but the most responsive to change." I wonder if he saw the positions that Africans held today would he like how I used his quote. Probably not! Because this proved without a doubt that we were the strongest species. The African American mentality has suffered the most drastic changes other than the American Indian and the German Jew. Still, I ask why they have both been compensated for their pain, and we haven't!

Anthony T. Browder wrote, "Your philosophy determines your actions" my thoughts on that quote are as follows. I think that as African Americans, we have no cultural philosophy, it was taken away with slavery's chain, thus creating a people that are lost, and the Europeans took every advantage they could from this. They still are today! In 1883 the court ruled that the 14th Amendment prohibited state governments from discriminating against people because of race, but it did not restrict private organizations or individuals from doing so. Thus railroads, hotels, restaurants, theaters, etc., could legally practice segregation. This is another pivotal point when slavery's chains were replaced with desperation. We were given a false sense of freedom. In this chapter, I tried to focus on the rules, legalities, and some points about slavery; now, let's discuss the life of a slave.

CHAPTER 6
AMERICA

NECESSITY

Many royal lineages were captured as slaves according to African tradition. Leaders and people were all sharing one common lot. This sense of oneness applied to all members of the tribe. This oneness is the reason why chiefs and kings would greedily secure prisoners of war by attacking other tribes. You still ask why? It's simple only a savage king or chief would sell his own bloodline into enslavement. This divide gave the Europeans much joy because this agitated bickering between tribes served two purposes. It kept them paid, and it kept the Africans divided. This hatred between the tribes derived from manipulative European games and the Blacks with insignificant tribal warfare and feuds. A year before the arrival of the celebrated mayflower.

One hundred and thirteen years before George Washington's birth and two hundred and 44 years before the Emancipation Proclamation. The first slave ships sailed into the Harbor of Jamestown, Virginia. This event is remembered as a powerful beginning, but we as African Americans must remember this. That was not the beginning of Black America but the real beginning of America's rise to power. This is where this Great Nation crawled on our ancestors' backs! This is where White supremacy was planted in the soil of America. This is where millions of Africans lost their ancestral lineage, thus weakening the Black Race forever and aligning us with servitude, savagery, and a lower status in humanity. America was founded on racism, oppression, and an unequal fight for liberty. America only prospered with the oppression and enslavement of the Indian an

African Race. African slaves built the great United States! They brainwashed us into believing we were inferior. Even with religion, they processed us to believe that the White man was God. Crazy when the Jews in the Bible were dark tone and curly-haired. Why? Why did they change his face to blond hair and blue eyes if race didn't matter?

Truth be told, Africans were bought to the United States to serve as a catalyst, as an economic stepping stone in an industrial revolution. When that revolution slowed, slaves were thought to be no longer needed. Strangely the slave trade wasn't just done by Whites, but the Spanish, the Dutch, and Portuguese all aided the European in the deception. The Blacks sold Blacks for brandy and new weapons to kill or capture the other tribes that the Europeans needed to be moved or enslaved. (pimping them). Europeans reasons for entering Africa first were gold and diamonds. This continues today, yet then they found something extremely more profitable. Slaves!

William Hawkins made probably the first recorded transatlantic African trading voyages from England to Ghana (Africa) then to Brazil, thus profiting. He then got the first financial backer from Queen Elizabeth in 1561 for the slave trade. His son John Hawkins changed the trading voyage to what we know now as the triangular slave routes that enslaved millions. Hawkins was the first to do this on record. By taking three ships to Sierra leone in 1562 to capture Africans to sell in Spain. However, Hawkins just didn't trade slaves; he was also a major slave raider. He burned and killing thousand, creating chaos in Africa for years.

Meanwhile, things were getting worse in the newfound America, and nothing seemed could help. Until the discovery of tobacco! Spain at that time held a tight grip on the tobacco trade until a thief, crook, and sailor. John Rolfe stole a seed of an exclusive strain of tobacco. This Industrial theft marked a new day and also an economic revolution in America. Rolfe then went to Virginia and grew his strain called (Varina). He also named his plantation Varina (which still grows tobacco to this very day). By 1612 Virginians had found their breadwinner, its cash crop, tobacco, instead of shipping olives for the rich English. They supplied loads of cheap tobacco, thus changing the United states future. They now had a product, uncultivated land, and a hungry market. They need one thing, workers! In 1616 Virginia's Governor Thomas Dale started private land acquisitions. He offered a hundred acres only if they were company men. Still, Virginia's new settler got 50 acres. With all this land, marketability with the English. Virginia grew thousands of acres of tobacco. It was hard and very difficult. The planters desperately needed workers for this task. The first contracts for indentured servants were written in Sep. 17,1619 with the Berkley hundred in 1619. Virginia Colony Secretary Jhonny Pory wrote to England. "our principle wealth consistent in servants. "With that letter, it was revealed to all English that in the new world, workers were capital assets. John Rolfe was low-key and a very private person in the financial history of Virginia. America hides the story of his theft, Yet most people remember him for marrying the daughter of Pamunkey; he was the Chief Powtain. We all know the story of the beautiful Pocahontas. Shocked now, right! Well, let me tell you more. Rolfe also was one of the first to document the sale of slaves in America. An estimated 10.7 million Africans were enslaved an estimated 1.8 million unknown died at sea. Some may say out of those millions, only 49,300 landed in the USA. So, for every two million enslaved, over a million died! Why? Diseases, starvation, and mostly self-respect! A little-known fact in European history books both tells that the captured Africans preferred death over slavery!

Still, those 500,000 or so Africans were symbolically only the seed. By 1860 there would be an outstanding 4 million Africans in the USA! The great racist president Thomas Jefferson once quoted, "Each birth was an addition to capital." Sad but true wealth regardless. A slave child sold in the market or kept on the plantation created money in this new land. Surely the four million slaves were a great economic expansion. Four million free workers! Peter Woods, who wrote the book "The Black Majority in 1974," Wrote a study of seventeenth-century showed South Carolina was one of a number of works that move the debt back toward social and economic condition. "Woods demonstrated that Blacks and Whites often worked together on relatively equal terms during the 17th century in America. Those early years of settlement were crucial to the forming of this country. Racism, in other words, did not intentionally shape the relationship between the Black and White; rice cultivation expanded the gap tremendously in the Carolinas. Thus, creating a deeper economical divide. The growth of the southern economy was chained directly to the productivity of the capitalized womb. Life was not like gone with the wind, were slave was never sad, they were dressed in clothing, and loved by their masters. Blacks were like cattle! The southern financial system depended on slavery! Let me give you an example of the southern economy. Planters mortgaged their plantations' livestock on slaves. If the crops failed, the slave could be taken by the bank and sold, thus expanding the bank portfolio in stocks, bonds. Then they were sold to an investor in New York, London, and everywhere else in the world.

Everyone benefited from American slavery, not just the American Whites! The world! From a financial point of view, New York benefited mostly. How? Because New York Banks captured, the credit and foreign exchange generated by slave's credit today is still money. Even the famous president Thomas Jefferson by funding the renovation of Monticello with slaves. Mortgaging the labor force that did the work. He was such a capitalist and greedy businessman. That after he died, the debt of his estate was outrageous. His slaves and property were sold at auctions. Even today, there is a host of fortune 500 corporations that excelled to greatness because of slavery's free labor. EXAMPLE: Hartford Insurance Companies, including the existing Aetna, sold policies to slave shoppers and owners even after the laws prohibited the slave trade. Northerners financed the legal slave trade in Cuba and Brazil. It was simple slaves were collateral, a banking account. A walking bank, most definitely. Slaves were used as saving accounts for the financially struggling Southern American economy. Take a second in, and let's do little currency history. In 1804, the penny wasn't in common circulation. The Spanish Pollar or Peso was even in shortage.

Therefore, until the discovery of gold in California in 1848. The American slave was used in the south as collateral or as a staple of wealth. So, if enslaved people were money, enslaved children were bonds or interests. What's crazy is we still are today with the prison system. This is no joke! This horrific detail even is in our constitutions. The three-fifths clause allows for counting three-fifths of a person's bond to service, i.e., slave. A slave!

Determining a State Representative in the House of Representation was especially designed to allow the south to vote strictly on the wealth of slaves. Therefore, making captive African Americans a story of political wealth. This vote was signaling to the south that the more slaves you had, the more political persuasion you had. Fanny Kemble Quoted the word of a very disgusted Carolinians in her 1838-39 Journal.

"I'll tell you why abolitionist is Impossible! because every healthy Negro can fetch a thousand dollars in Charleston at this moment."

Slave labor was the artisans of the colonial and antebellum south. How can we move forward without knowing that slaves built this nation that feeds off us still? Slaves built the White House, US Capitol, transformed forest, cut lumber out of animal-infested swamps. Slaves worked the iron mines, mined tunnels, built turnpikes, printing presses, and dug the hot salt mines. Slaves cleaned and repaired southern streets and canals. They built almost all the railroads in the South. With that, all said how they cannot still be rich today. How can the oppressors' bloodline not benefit financially off the money for generations? Just as we, the children of the slaves, are still suffering for generations.

After the importation of slaves was banned, Lewis Hughes wrote in 1861, "Virginia was the mother of slavery" Because, at the time, Virginia was the number one supplier of slaves. The South was booming! The largest in the south was New Orleans; the second was Natchez, Mississippi. Slave owners formed the majority of the southern political class. They also had control over southern states' government from top to bottom. South Carolina, the most proud of the slave-riddled democracy, stood tall in every anti-slavery legislation. In 1860, the southern states' legal system was organized around the unlucky enslavement of African people. They were not only dependent, but they thrived on the slave system. They would have never been successful without the slaveholder's profits. At the time of succession, two-third of the millionaires in this country lived in the souths, slave states. With most of their wealth in the forms of slaves. The souths economy was entirely built on slaves! Financially nothing surpassed slavery; it even passed cotton and tobacco. "The south's 1860 population of 3,953,742 enslaved people comprised or made valuable an estimated four billion dollars." Four billion dollars in 2010 would be the equivalent of over a hundred billion dollars. "During that time, slavery was twenty times the value of the entire crop of tobacco and cotton and 17.5 times all the gold and silver in circulation in the USA." The Confederate states knew that if slavery stopped, it would cripple them. The north also understood that crippling them would cripple the united states. Quoted, "we must either submit to degradation and to the loss of property worth over four billion in money, or we must succeed from the Union." Emancipation destroyed an entire financial system. "The security of millions of dollars in labor and debt would just walk away." This would destroy the wealthy 2 percent. In my opinion, emancipation destroyed an entire financial system in the form of property, which is why it was, in my opinion, also that it was just America's second revolution. This Revolution didn't bring freedom totally. It brought smoke screens like sharecropping and other tricks. An important fact, if only the freed Blacks would not have agreed to this ploy. It would have changed the face of the south completely! According to Article 1, Section 9 of the United States Constitution read. "The migration or importation of such persons as any of the states now existing shall think proper to admit, shall not be prohibited by the Congress before the year one thousand eight hundred and eight, but a tax or duty may be imposed on such importation, not exceeding ten dollars for each person." Slaves were substituted with the importation of a person. Strangely, this part contains the only date in the Constitution and price. The ten dollars just was set because they knew with that number. The slave trade could not be taxed out totally and also to show the government that money could be made for the federal budget. While showing a face of kindness and help, our government has never had good intentions in mind for slaves. This tactic always has and still exists as to their way of doing business even today. And yes, they are still making money off our economical enslavement. Even the importation of slave's stoppage was politically motivated to favor their pockets. One of my favorite authors Ned and Constance Sublet, wrote in "The American Slave Coast" that their slave-owning politicians loom large in our narrative as principle enablers of the territorial expansion of slavery, and consequently, of the Slave Breeding Industry." Thomas Jefferson, Andrew Jackson, and James Polk. All three were slave traders and like slave owners. Their wealth was primarily stored in the form of captive human beings. So their entire financial makeup consisted depended on slavery. Their political, social, and financial growth depends on the price and population of slaves. Economically restricting the importation or captive by keeping the African trade closed would kill the economy and supply. That's when they just started to breed them like cattle, selling them to the needy south. President Jefferson owned over a thousand human beings in his lifetime. No matter what, he always planned for slavery expansion. He wasn't the only one. The highly acclaimed general Andrew Jackson, before his presidency, planned on slavery's expansion. With the removal of the native Americans in Florida. He did this all under the cover of the War of 1812. This still helped the slave trade. President Polk, the known racist and slave owner, lobbied the Mexican War in Texas to expand. Polk was even said to buy slaves from his White House office! He did this in hopes of building his nest egg for retirement. All while he worked as president, expanding slavery's borders. Jackson, Jefferson, and Polk all used their slave wealth to pay for their political aspirations. An all would become Presidents of the United States. Asking yourself this now, Why would these men change their wealthy lives and way of living to help slaves out? They didn't; they lined theirs and their friend's pockets just as every other president has done since America's birth. As leaders, as presidents, they had the wrong intentions!

Our government has literally been against us since Elizabeth, the first female slave, landed in Virginia in shackles. By these presidents lobbying for an end to importation played two roles. It silenced the anti-slavery groups making them believe they were helping their cause. The second was money! It skyrocketed slave sales, value, and breeding. Forced mating was then sufficiently carried out by our government strictly for the financial betterment of themselves and the United States. The so-called founding fathers' presidents/slave owners sought to dream of a world where they could breed Negroes and sell them worldwide! During James K. Polk's presidency, his brother-in-law Robert W. Campbell, who watched over his plantation, ensured and promoted that. "He would purchase young slave girls" With the purpose of force breeding them with his older male slaves. Our African queens had no choice! The American government made captive laborers into financial products, merchandise, cash, productive capital, collateral. Then even at the end of the chains, stocks, and bonds.

<u>FOUNDATION</u>

Break the Chains

"We must get over the plantation pride about the numbers of Negro's in the Big House."

Albert B. Clegge Jr.

Beginning just before the establishment of the English colonies in North America. A time when the first known Documented Groups of Enslaved Africans came to what we call the United States. I have stated already that African slavery was introduced to Iberia by Portugal in 1441! During this time, slavery was associated with Spain and Portugal. Blacks in England at that time were called Blackamoors. Strangely During this time, Martin Luther King came on the scene with his theory that freedom was closely associated with reading the Bible in his language. Slavery was closely associated with the Catholic Rituals. This made it easier for them to control the unruly Africans.

"Slavery was not the state of love and confidence between Master and Slave that we often see pictured in books."

Judge O. Temple 1904

Servitude and slavery were very different! The first known example was "Boch" by Olaudah. He served in both situations. He served unwillingly. He was in servitude in Africa. Then the British captured him in 1700. He then got the platform to express himself.

He stated, "When I was in servitude in Africa, I was treated as an extended family member with humanity and care. European slavery was different. I was beaten, starved, even seen men raped."

European slavery was barbaric; rape was used to de-maculate the men. They would send the worst ones to Jamaica to the seasoning plantations. There they would rape the baddest, biggest male slave in front of everyone! Multiple times to get their mental message through to the youth. This is why in my theory, the Jamaican Culture frowns down so viciously on homosexuality to this day.

Lizere Barnett, a Centenarian who was interviewed in the 1930s, stated, "I heard the awful cries of the slaves, the flesh would be cut in great gaps, and the maggots would get in them, and the slaves would scream in misery." These beatings and other tortures are too numerous to mention. This process could kill, and a lot did die. All this was done to psychologically scar the slaves.

The Willie Lynch letter stated, "We reversed nature by burning and pulling one civilized Nigger apart or bullwhipping the other to the point of death." (All in the female's presence)

This process left her mentally alienated, being left alone, and unprotected with the male image destroyed. Left her mind in a frozen, psychological state of independence. She will then raise her male and female offspring in reversed roles for fear of the young male's life. She then will psychologically train him to be mentally weak and dependent but still physically strong. (A good slave!) You have now gotten the Black female out front trying to protect the scared male with this move. "The Willie Lynch letter also stated, "Before the Breaking process, we had to be on alert and on guard at all times" After the Breaking Process. "We could now sleep soundly for now out of frozen fear this woman. The Black Woman. Stands guard for us." Strangely anyone that has been to a correctional institution will tell you mostly Black women run the facilities. "Continually through the Breaking of uncivilized Niggers, by throwing the Nigger Female savage into a frozen, psychological state of independence by killing the protection of her male image, creating a submissive dependent mind of the Nigger male slave, we have created an orbiting cycle that turns on its axis forever unless a phenomenon occurs." With this quote, I thought to myself about Malcolm X, Martin, Medgar, even myself. We all must be a phenomenon! Because each male that stands up is not in their plans. "This phenomenon occurring because the mind has a strong drive to correct and recorrect itself over a period of time. If it can touch some substantial original historical base. Yet the best way to deal with this happening is to shave off the brutes mentality, mental history and create a multiplicity of phenomenon or illusions so that each illusion will twirl in its own orbit, something akin to floating balls in a vacuum. The purpose of which is to create a diversified division of labor." They wanted us to be distracted by drugs, cars, clothes, etc. So why would our government help us? Why would they try to change our situation or mentality? I once read, "If you take a slave and you teach him about your language, he will know all of your secrets, and then he is no more a slave." With that said, we have to learn the language of America! We have to learn capitalism, economics, business, law, and politics. We have to learn the language of America! We have to learn to progress. Which they also tried since our arrival to prevent.

In 1849 Virginia legal codes stated a free person, who dared assemble with Negroes to instruct them to read and write, could receive a jail sentence of up to six months and a fine of $100. The enslaved that tried to learn lost fingers or worst.

In the 1920s and '30s, Europeans depicted Africans as cannibals, barbarians, savages, and animals with bones in their noses, Black pots boiling eating White people. Strangely in European culture, there is more evidence showing that they did cannibalism. Think for a second, if you will. In a frozen area from where Europeans are said to have evolved, this area with no food. What do you eat? Now, if you are African, with thousands of animals, fruits, vegetables, etc. Why would you eat another African? You wouldn't! There is evidence of more cannibalism in European culture than in any African culture.

In Virginia in the 1600s and Europe in the 1400s. Vlad the Impaler was idolized for drinking blood and eating people. So why give us that stigmata? This was done to help further promote the race as savages because this would ease the backlash of their brutal treatment of African people. European tactics like lynching or rape were only used as control devices to keep the slave's mentality in place, correcting the phenomenon. Don't get me wrong; it was 75% hate and 25% mental warfare. This is why they made lynching's a spectacle in town. This was done to show other Whites they were still in control. Lynchings would be announced at churches like birthdays or graduations. They would have big parties; they would sell raffle tickets for different items. These savages felt entitled to kill Black people! They felt prideful, respected, and cavalier to kill Africans. They would bring the whole family out to parks, lay out blankets, eat, drink, and pick a nigga to hang. Thus, having a picnic? Slavery was terrible for African men yet unimaginable for African women. Their terrors were brutal and unthinkable.

Harriet Jacobs wrote, "Slaveholders have been doing enough to enact that the child shall follow the conditions of the mother, not the father." Why? Because they would openly rape our women with impurity and impregnate them with Caucasian bastard seeds. Sojourner, truth born in New York in 1797, was said to have exposed her breast to a proslavery crowd in Indiana while shouting, "My breast have suckled many a White baby, to the exclusion of my offspring!" Which was and still today a horrific thing for any woman to do. Imagine taking care of your rapist, molester, and abuser's children before your own.

"Paetus Sequitus" was the legal term: the status of the newborn follows the status of the womb. Fathers passed inheritance down mothers passed slavery down for mulatto children. This ensured a steady form of pleasure and money for the slave owners and torturers. This meant more terror and pain for African women. Who had no legal say so on their children's lives? Savilla Burrel, a slave from Winnsboro, South Carolina, stated, "Old masa wus de daddy of some mulatto children re'lation is wid de mother of dese children is what give so much grief to mistress, de neighbors would talk about a trader my mistress would sell all dem children away from dey mothers to a trader my mistress would cry about dat." Slave owners even regarded their own children as property which is unthinkable. They would sell the mulatto as soon as possible, getting the children out of their sight in their wives. This building of slavery became more of an elaborate, radical thing as generations on both sides began to grow up with slavery's normalities. For most, it just was a part of life and soon law.

In 1700 the casual killing law said, "If you killed someone Black to correct them, it would not be considered a felony. This law was put in place to protect White women. Why? Because they would beat newborn mulatto children, born by rape into slavery to death. It pained them knowing the children were the offspring of the husband's affairs. Still, most slave owners felt, as quoted, "Crossbreeding niggers meant taking so many drops of good White blood an putting them into as many nigger women as possible, varying the drops by the various tones that you want an, then letting them breed with each other until the circle of color appeared as you desire." This is crazy!

In 1865 they stopped trafficking slaves laws were passed, but the American Cotton plantations still needed the slaves, and now more of them. So now breeding farms were invented. The two biggest states that had these farms were Maryland and Richmond, VA. They were breeding Africans like cattle. They didn't care if it was mothers, sons, fathers, daughters, or brothers and sisters. They forced them to breed under the pretense of torture. This is where the term (motherfucker) came from. Maryland, the second biggest in the north were just as active. In the trade of breeding or greater. Maryland ports alone, specifically Baltimore, shipped out 11,966 people for whom records exist between 1818 and 1853. A well-known number of others before their time. America was never meant to be for us! It was meant to be used on us for them to prosper.

The evidence is conclusive; we see this even today how we are treated in politics, entertainment, and a host of other systems. So why would they help us! They imported us from Africa now; they were breeding us like cattle. Then distributing us around like property. At this point, after the laws were passed on importation. Slaves bought in Virginia and Maryland would be walked in groups called coffles. The dictionary definition of coffee is "a train of beast or men fastened together. The slaves often sang to hide their pain as they traveled. Sis Sahackled stated, "Dey all just singing and shoutin make all de noise dey can tryin to hide de sorrer in dey hearts, an cover up de cries, and moans of dem leving behind." Women with babies in hand were in a cruel situation. To a slave, babies weren't worth much money and slowed travel time down a lot. There is a story by a slave named William Wells Brown. He recalled a young African mother traveling with a child. From most likely rape, being transported with this coffle. The child grew cross with the travel and kept crying. He stated the woman tried to keep the child quiet but could not. After the next day of travel that morning. The child was still upset and crying. The slave trader, Mr. Walker, walked up to the trembling young slave girl and told her to give the child to him. Though shaken, she obeyed in fear for her and the child's safety. Brown recalls, "He took the child by one arm, as you would a cat by the leg. Walked into the house and said to the lady, Madame, I will make you a present of this little nigger! It keeps such a noise I cannot bear it." Just like that, the mother never saw her child or the child his mother again. "Wow!

LIBERATION

"You don't get liberated through morality; you get liberated through power."

Kwame Tore

The pro-Black and strong liberator Marcus Garvey once said, "There must be a sincere desire and longing on the part of those people to be returned to the father's land." I was taught as a child that to learn something is to be liberated from it. The powers in the United States understood early they couldn't mistreat other people, Races Cultures simply because most of their home countries would protect them, well, everyone except the Africans. We were victims of racism in the USA like never before. Take, for instance, the killings of the Italians in 1890. In 1890 some Italian immigrants got lynched in New Orleans. Italy almost went to war with the USA behind the lynchings. The USA was embarrassed and begged Italy for forgiveness. They publicly apologized and paid for the funerals of the Dead Italians. Yes, you did read that it's true. They paid for their funerals! With that said, our Government understood that lynching was wrong, yet they let many privileged Whites lynch hundreds of Black with Immunity, and nothing was done! Was it our fault as African Americans, or Africans fault for not coming to our aid like Italy?

In early wars fought on the United States, soil Africans have sided with whoever promised freedom. This is still being done now, yet politically with promises of better health care, housing, pay, and other tricks used by politicians. In Saint Dominique, Black Generals fought with the Spanish against the French, The Great Toussaint Leveture. They ended up crossing over to the French once France had Declared Emancipation with North America. The enslaved of Virginia defeated to the British in the War of Independence and the war of 1812. They then helped the union against the racist Confederates. Happily killing their once bold oppressors along the way. A letter by a Fredericksburg, Virginia Paper in 1800 declared that. "If we will keep a ferocious monster in our country, we must keep them in chains." That they did, and we are still in chains today mentally, emotionally, and economically. It revealed the plan, the thought process, and real intentions of America's Forefathers with that statement. The people wanted to keep us in chains! Mary turner of Quitman, GA, went through this. Mary's husband Hayen Turner got into some trouble in nearby Valdosta, GA. She went to the jail to help him, and instead, the hanging party took her. They led her to a nearby Folsom Bridge, where she was stripped naked. They beat her, strung her up, and as she slowly died, they noticed her stomach moving. She was pregnant! They then cut out the baby and stomped it to Death! Nothing was done to the people that did this; where was the help? Where were the apologies from the US Government to help pay for her funeral?

Marcus Garvey said, "You can be educated in soul, vision, and as well in mind to see your enemy and know him as a part of the complete education of man." True lasting active esteem only comes from inside. That is why people call it self-esteem. The original design of the Statue of Liberty was a Black Female! Why? It was said that the French artist dedicated this statue to represent the end of slavery. The original model has a Negro's nose an Negro features. She also had chains on her hands and feet. When America receive it, they wanted the facial features changed. They also removed the chains. The French artist protested yet changed the face into the Patron face of manifest destiny. The chains were removed off the hands, yet they left them on her feet.

Why did he choose the Black female? Symbolically I feel because the African female was the root of the oppression. If you control the womb and the woman, you control the offspring! Thus, creating a generational unbalance between White and Black. Ned and Constance Sublet stated, "The reason slaves could not legally be created equal was not merely that appropriating one hundred percent of their labor was wildly profitable, nor is it the many forms of comfort and pleasure they afforded. Their owners, nor even the owners, routinely expressed fear that if freed. The Blacks would do to the Whites, what the Whites had done to them." That showed two things in my thought process. It shows fear and knowing remorse for their actions. They were remorseful because they knew they were wrong and feared they would receive karma back for the wrongs they committed against the slaves. They feared the greatness of freedom would empower us, which they knew it would, and it did! Rebellions by the slaves existed where ever there was slavery in every era of slavery. Because everywhere, the enslaved were always at war with the conditions, with the oppressors with slavery. A rebellion started in Africa on slave ships, plantations, towns, and cities.

In 1831 Nat Turner, a slave preacher, led a band of African American slaves. Armed with guns and axes, they went from house to house in South Hampton County, Virginia, killing 60 White men, women, and children. They eventually were overpowered by State and Federal troops. Born in 1820 into slavery in Maryland, Harriet Tubman was destined to be a fighter for slavery.

In 1849 when her master died, she escaped to Philadelphia to avoid being sold out of state. Over the next ten years, she assisted over three hundred slaves to escape Maryland plantations. Starting with her own family. Harriet had the strength, courage, and knowledge to understand that once you get a route to freedom. It is then your obligation to save your family! Then your tribe, then your family, and tribe are obligated to save other tribes and families.

Herbert Aptheker, in 1943, found records of approximately two hundred and 50 revolts, conspiracies, and plots in the history of African slavery.

Break the Chains

Take, for instance, a 22-year-old Ova judge. She was Martha Washington's personal servant. She escaped from the Presidential First Lady of the United States in Philadelphia in 1796 after learning she would be given away as a wedding gift. She later married a free Black man in Portsworth, New Hampshire, and managed to avoid falling prey to the multiple attempts of recapture that George Washington made until he died in 1799. History has forgotten about all the Great Blacks that are not mentioned in everyday literature. History forgot Bass Reeves. Bass Reeves was one of the worst Black slave revolvers ever, but he is seldom mentioned simply because of his greatness. Bass beat up his master, went to Oklahoma, where he was then recruited by law enforcement. They wanted him badly because he knew how to speak Greek, Mischa, and a couple of other Indian languages. He went on to bring in 3,000 fugitives as a bounty hunter. His legend was replaced in Hollywood by a White man on film, which we all know as the Lone Ranger. Rebellions, no matter how small they were indifferent instances. They all were extraordinary! They were effective at bringing the war on slavery forward! The Stone Rebellion of 1739, the alleged New York Conspiracy in 1741, Gabriel's Conspiracy 1800, The German Coast Rebellion 1831. All of these rebellions, wars were great news to the enslaved and a portrait of a nightmare for the slave owners. African Americans had to go through the nightmare to get liberated. We had to go through the storm to get to a better day! We had to gain control over our families, wives, and children and teach them that life, love, and respect go a long way. Teach them that respect for your community, family, and culture will lead generations to freedom. Just as Harriet Tubman held a responsibility to her family, community, and culture, You Do as Well!!!

CHAPTER 7
SLAVERY AFTERMATH

MIGRATION

I once read in a book about business management. "To learn to fly, you have to jump first." After the civil war, there were four million free Black people with no education, housing, and healthcare. Instead of helping these broken, beaten, and misused people. They issued the Black codes, slave codes, and peonage. My opinion of this madness is that the North should have destroyed then rebuilt the racist South. This maybe would not have stopped the spread of the southern hate philosophy and White supremacy. This maybe would have brought America to a different stage today. While Americans' fear of African Americans' freedom was strongly caused by the elimination of slavery. This also caused them to formulate a bigger and better economic plan. To the south, slaves were an asset; as soon as slavery was over, slaves became a liability. They even tried to send us back to Africa. After they had used us to clear the swamps, forests and laid the groundwork for America. Our great government was all for it. Congress funded the American colonization society. Amazingly it didn't work. Paul Cuffie led and paid for the first Black to Africa movement in 1815. Negotiating to send Blacks back to Sierra Leone. They thought of us as Refugees! When they were the ones that kidnapped us and brought us to this land. Still, the difference between an immigrant and a Refugee is that our Government grants assistance for immigrants legally, and Refugees don't get that welcoming aid. Still, these Africans thrived and withstood the mistreatment and degradation that the Whites put in their paths. Painstakingly the successful Blacks were killed first after slavery's dismantling. Why were they killed? Because of simple jealousy and hate!

Ida B. Wells wrote once of the pains of her best friends getting lynched, that ran a successful business in Memphis. They tried stagnating us economically still, and since then, this economic stagnation has been a top priority since Africans arrived in the United States. Until we, as African Americans, realized that this was and still is a capitalistic economy. We built America! Africans have founded many cities. Take, for instance, Buffalo, which was founded by a Black man Joe Hodges. He was once quoted as to have said he went to Buffalo because the Native Americans were better than the Whites. In 1827 freed African slaves migrated to NY and purchased land that would come to be known as Seneca Village. The name Seneca was short for Senegal. This was a place known for helping the escaped, freed, and homeless Africans that migrated to New York. It was rumored to be a part of the Underground Railroad. As word soon spread about their help, more and more Blacks started to move there from everywhere. The then New York Mayor confiscated the land under Eminent Domain. He forcefully removed all the Blacks! The last African family was removed in 1857. The land where Africans set out to make an Epicenter for freed slaves was taken and renamed Central Park! Yes, Central Park! African slaves fled the south in droves to Chicago, Maryland, New York, anywhere they would have ease of painful southern slave life. Migration brought freedom from slavery and some Southern White Supremacist rules. Yet, it also brought new challenges with new legal codes and policies designed to keep us docile!

POPULATION CONTROL

"Power is the ability to define reality and to make others accept your definition as their own."

Wade W. Nobles

The most valuable possession to the Black Race in America is Black Children. They are undoubtedly our people's greatest potential resources. With the Africans future being vigorously threatened, our children's future has been threatened as a whole. Frances Cress Weisin said, "Any meaningful discussion of the survival of the future of Black people must be directed upon Black peoples plan for the motivational development of all Black children." I believe this with 100% certainty that he was right! Simply said, without the Black seeds, there is no Black future! In slavery's time, castration was done as punishment or fear of a certain slave. During slavery, they wanted us to reproduce as livestock does to produce profit. That meant more capital. After slavery, they wanted, looked for, and tried various ways to keep us from producing. Population Control was also a result of envy. Why? Because the White Man can only make one kind of color child White! The Black Man can make many colors. Frances Galton was considered to be the father of Eugenics and Was renowned in his field. He came from a wealthy family that gained their wealth off the slave trade. He was the first cousin of popular racist Charles Darwin. Darwin's Theory was that the African was after the monkey, yet before the White man in evolution. Therefore, Galton believed this also. He believed in decreasing the African Race that he also felt were inferior in stock and increasing the stock in the race that were not. He took his cousin Darwin's philosophy to heart and thought and put them into practice. He believed strongly that Caucasians were the highest level of primates on Earth. To White supremacists, this was law, and the theories of Eugenics solved the Negro Problem. Galton was quoted as saying. "I do not join in the belief that the African is our equal in heart and brain, and I believe that if we can in a fair way poses ourselves of his services, we have an Equal Right to utilize them to our advantage." Charles Darwin Book "The Origin of Species" Original name was. "The Origin of Species by means of Natural Selection of Preservation of Favored race in the Struggle of life." In this book, he wrote, "At some future period, not very distant as measured by centuries. The civilized race of man will almost certainly exterminate and replace the savage race throughout the world. The book between man and his nearest allies will be wider, for it will intervene between man and his nearest allies will be wider. For it will intervene between man in a more civilized state and some Ape as low as a Baboon, instead of as now between the Negro or Australian and the Guerilla."

Although a great scientist, Charles Darwin was indeed a great racist and indeed very wrong; still, this sounded very alarming and scary to the wealthy White elites. Frances Gatlin wrote in 1873 after American slavery was supposedly over. "The average Negro poses to little intellect, self-reliance, and self-control to make it possible for them to sustain burgess of any Respectable Civilization without a large measure of external guidance and support." This theory was quickly set aside as the ex-slaves started to prosper. Darwin didn't oppose slavery until it had ended. Galton's first try at race depopulation was positive Eugenics, which was the process of Whites overpopulating the world, thus overpowering the Black race with White babies. That didn't work! Why? Because the Blacks were reproducing faster than the Whites. Next, they tried negative Eugenics to create an environment where the Blacks would be severely limited in their childbirths. Thereby committing race suicide. They couldn't promote this way of eugenics publicly as they could with positive Eugenics. Instead, they reverted to their old tactics. The same negative propaganda was used to promote slavery's laws. They called the Blacks feeble-minded, unfit, immoral, criminal. All to make society believe they were doing the right thing by killing Blacks. Amazingly the same corporations that made millions off the backs of slaves now were ready to spend millions to get rid of them. These Elitist were the ones that adapted the Eugenics methodology. Simply because they didn't want to give up or lose their rich lifestyles. The problem with positive eugenics was they couldn't stand out publicly and say. "We want to kill Black babies!" They had to hide their faces yet funnel their money into the right places, projects, and people's hands. Then came their front runner. Miss Margaret Sanger.

Margaret Sanger was so proud of her hate that she gave speeches on race control at KKK Rallies in the South. She would brag to her rich Northern friends that the southerners would always invite her to more Events because of her strong outlooks on the Negro. Margaret Sanger would later become one of the co-founders of the American Birth Control leagues and the founder of the Birth Control Review. She became the face of Population Control! She would join with the American Elitist, making this platform the driving force behind the Eugenics Movement. In one of the letters to her fellow Eugenic Board Members, she stated, "We are paying for and submitting to the dictation of an ever-increasing, spanning class of Human Beings, Who never should have been born at all." These powerful men set in motion millions of deaths of Black children that were on welfare.

Simply under the threat of taking away food surplus. Our government willingly did this under the banner of helping us using the same games the slave owners used. They claimed this was done to prevent feeble-minded people from reproducing. It's crazy because only God knows what a child will become when he grows up. They sterilized young girls as young as nine years old, preventing them from having children simply because they were Black!

U.S. Supreme Court Justice Oliver Wendell Holmes wrote in a letter on the sterilization laws in Virginia to President Roosevelt in 1927. "It is better for all the world if instead of waiting to execute offspring for crime or to let them starve for their Imbecility, society can prevent them who are manifestly unfit from continuing their kind. Three generations of imbeciles are enough." Roosevelt would later appoint Holmes to the Supreme Court. In 1927 Buck vs. Bell came into play; it was about the sterilization of Black women. There were at least 60,000 Black women that were on record as sterilized in this process. Sixty thousand! Ten years later, in a later report, there were an additional 150,000 women were added. Wow! Dr. Benjamin Hayes once said, "The Black man has never been a competition, but has always have been subservient to the White race. Just as long as he. (the Black man) Has remained subservient, his position is secure, and just so soon as he became a competitor, his fate then is sealed." This mentality was the effect of multiple negative forces. Multiple centuries of mental enslavement. They wanted us to stay docile, subservient even though our country's great leaders fought both tooth and nail to keep us in bondage. This hate This disease of racism is like any other disease. It travels and affects other people, some more than others.

In 1934 Adolf Hitler wrote the Eugenics Board Members and praised one, particularly Mr. Leon Whitney, for his writings on slavery. One of Whitney's quotes stated, "If we could purge the country of our typical slum element in city and country, what harm could be done." The Nazis were normal allies to the United States when it came to killing Blacks and forced sterilizations. They did experiments on Blacks also not just the Jews. Blacks were the first to receive their negative impact on the world. In 1944 Robert Lay wrote a book called. (The German Labor Front) He stated that. "The Jew diseased ridden parasite, the offspring of White men an Negro, this human swamp would destroy the Aryan Race." Hitler was fascinated with the agenda to kill the Jews. He wrote in his book. (Mine Kamp) "The Jew was responsible for bringing the Negro into the Rhineland; it suits the purpose of the cool, calculating Jew who would use this means of introducing a process of Basterdation in the very center of the European continent and by infecting the whole White race with the blood of an inferior stock would destroy the foundation of its independent existence." In my theory, Adolf Hitler wanted to impress the Americans. As a result, he killed 50 million Jews. Ok, Ok, Let's not get too far ahead focusing on the end results yet let me carefully explain why this happened and how it is still relevant today. The USA Eugenics founder and followers applauded Hitler for his want to exterminate Negroes. Time Magazine wrote. "The leader of the German Nation, Hitler ably supported by Dr. Frick and guided by German anthropologist an social policy views, has been able to construct a comprehensive racial policy on population development and improvement." They admired Hitler's plan for killing Negroes, and Americans felt they were fighting the same cause. Dr. Clarence Gordon Campbell, the then

President of the American Eugenics research, wrote in the Time Magazine article. "The difference between the Jew and the Aryan is as insurmountable, as that between the Black and White. . .Germany has set a pattern which other nations must follow." They felt America should do the same and just kill all the Africans off. During an African experiment to exterminate the Blacks, Hitler called in Eugene Fischer. Fisher had been a leader in the Nazi Aryan African concentration camps where Blacks were rounded up and experimented on, executed, or used as slaves. Fisher was also one of the first Nazi supporters in those times to publicly fund eugenics Projects in New York. Fisher was quoted to have said, " Blacks are savages who only should be allowed to survive as long as they are of use to the Aryan race." Hitler wanted fisher to kill all the Blacks in the lands where the German would be in control. Fisher was also in charge of the Kiser William Institute, which the Rockefeller family founded. Here at the Kiser William Institute, many of the Nazi plans for race development were laid out and formed. How is it that the Rockefeller Legacy be so polished and celebrated by rappers when they were detrimental in the aid to killing Blacks and Jews? Yet Fisher wasn't the only help they had. Introducing now Lanthrop P. Stoddad. Stoddad was the American Birth Control League director, and he also sat on the American eugenics Board. He also was one of Adolf Hitler's biggest supporters. Stoddad wrote the heavily praised White supremacist book. "The Rising Tide of Color" He was noted as to have said, "Non-White races must be excluded from America, the Red and Black race. If not left to rule, yet left by themselves, they would revert back to savages or simply a simi savage state quickly. This book and his other book. "The Dragon cross" was wildly promoted to be held in the highest esteem by the KKK and other groups. Longthrop was also once believed to be a KKK member. He met with Adolph Hitler and Nazi madman Himelic Himler on December 19, 1939. After that Stoddads text would be used as study material in Nazi schools. This furthering the hate of the Blacks and Jews in the World.

1939 was also a memorable time in population control. In 1939 fellow Eugenics supporter and White supremacist Clarence Gamble aire to the Proctor and Gamble fortune, and members of the Carnegie family gave large amounts of money to these organizations. Both families wanted nothing more than to aid in the destruction of Black babies. In a letter from the now ever-popular racist Margret Singer to Clarence Gamble. She takes the time to answer and explain Gamble's questions about persuading the Black Ministers to help in their plans. "The minister's work is also important, and perhaps he should be trained by the federation as to our ideals and the goals we are trying to reach. We don't want the word to get out that we are trying to exterminate the Negro population. The minister is the person that can straighten that idea out if that ever occurs to any of the more rebellious members." They already had thought of the one percent that would buck the system. As always, the phenomenon used a weak link in our culture to aid in our defeat. The ever-looming compromisers.

The American Eugenics movement and the American Birth Control league cut ties with the Nazi movement in 1942. Why? After the world found out that Hitler was not just killing the Blacks but the Jews also. It was then exposed globally to how the Nazi camps were operated. Next, they felt they had to reinvent themselves for fear of bad publicity and world hatred. They now couldn't use words like control, race, development. So, they changed their name to who we all know as Planned Parenthood. Even the racist Margret singer cut ties with the Nazis. She stated, "I am not really a Eugenicist." It's funny how now she claimed planned parenthood was not a part of the organization, yet they still held some of the same offices as the Eugenicist. Jullian Huxely, a Planned Parenthood board member, said, "Force sterilization was needed for the Negro, and a lack of healthcare would also kill off their children."

One of Planned Parenthood's biggest supporters was Gunner Murdal, who wrote the book "American Dilemma." What made Murdal so special was his elitist friends. For instance, his book was funded by again the Rockefeller family and the Carnegie family. This book laid out the blueprint for African American population control. Murdal stated, "Commonly, it is considered a great misfortune for America that African slaves were ever imported. The presence of the Negro in America today is usually considered a plight of the nation." Painstakingly he was right. It was commonly felt that the Negro was no longer needed. Because the majority of the financial gain had already been met. Murdal also wrote, "All White Americans agree that if the must be eliminated. He must be eliminated slowly so as not to alert an individual Negro." This would be done so we all wouldn't know the plan. He also wrote, "Birth control facilities could be extended relativity more to Negro's than the Whites. Since Negroes are more concentrated in lower-income and low education classes." This is why we today see Planned Parenthood largely in African American neighborhoods versus rich White ones. After these groups have tried forced sterilization, birth control pills, sterilized water, jail coronavirus etc., they first found a major solution, legal abortions!

Since 1973 legal abortions have killed more Africans than AIDS, cancer, diabetes, heart disease, violent crimes, Coronavirus combined. Legal birth control! Every week more Black babies die at America's abortion clinics than people who died in the Vietnam war! Factually an African American baby is five times more at risk of being aborted than a White child. Take a look at the CDC stats before legal abortions. White women did eighty percent of all illegal abortions. That is why in 2019, the issue again was a big deal. They wanted White women to have babies. The numbers started to change. The most dangerous place for a Black child today is in the womb. Thus, putting the responsibility on the parents of African Americans. Even today, the racially motivated chain called Planned Parenthood is the largest in the United States.

In January 1973, the Supreme Court passed the abortion bill. Almost immediately, the (RCAR) "The Religious Coalition of Rights" To combat this. In a recorded conversation, even our president Richard Nixon was heard disgusting the extermination of Blacks. At what point is enough is enough! Systematically even today, we kill our own with less thought about what color we want to wear today or which dressing to add on a Salad. Blacks in America have lost the pride of having Black children. Having the bloodline pure and steady. Why do African men rather reproduce with other races? Blatantly trying to make an adorable-looking child with light skin, different color eyes. Other than having a child with strong-looking African features. Why? I will tell you why most stereotypical media or socialistic taboos of Black is ugly or bad. We have let them win with tricks and smoke screens. America has always survived off of Blacks suffering. When they need to make as many Negro babies became unpopular with slavery's end.

They deceived and are still deceiving plans to kill us slowly yet effectively. Still, we have added them in the fight because we still do drugs, gangbang, rob, steal, betray each other, and deal out death daily. It pains me that we don't have their sources to become fathers and successful family men. This is what we need!

SMOKESCREEN

"The most difficult thing to get people to do is to accept the obvious."

Dick Gregory

The great author Douglas A Blackman said, "Slavery was not a problem in America. It built America and was a solution to their financial, economic struggles! After slavery's so-called stoppage, the great White supremacists set out in many ways to stop and block our progress. One of the worst effects of early on economical oppression was the Freedmans Bank. After slavery, those hard-working Blacks worked and saved Their hard-earned money only to be robbed. How? Just by quitting! The Freedmans Bank closed the doors one day, keeping all of the people's money. This was a significant point of economical oppression and psychological in my point of view because even today, most Blacks don't trust banks with their money. This caused fear in the newly freed African American Community, so Blacks hid money in cans, mattresses or buried it. Some even bought property, still to have it taken in some kind of game played by money-grabbing systemic games. These instances caused Blacks mentally to not trust the system with their money, causing a divide in the economic growth of Black America. This divided not only broadened the gap between the elitist Whites but also the gap between the African Americans and the Negro. The African

Americans began to succeed and the Negro became stagnant. This lead to the African American class playing the same games on the Negro. If not for the Whites, the Whites would jail them etc. During their construction period after the Civil War, the Vatican stated that all western books on academia had to be first passed thru the Vatican system. Why was this? Either they wanted to make sure the higher-ups were doing a good job or to ensure educational White supremacy. The educational drive of the Black man is suffering from the backdraft of this. We, as Black Americans, still do not know the effect of our mindset or the mindset of the American people. Steve Biko said, "The greatest weapon in the hands of the oppressor is the oppressed. "We as Blacks have to have rules of integrity when it comes to money. Why? Because they expect you to kill, steal, die, and snitch on your whole race for money. It's called the illusion of inclusion. They used the Black burgess to simply control the other Blacks in slavery times. Back in slavery's time, a promotion for Blacks was a bad thing. You would be promoted to either sex slave or snitch. Sadly, the same thing goes on today! We have to fight!

We have to fight as they did in 1866. When (Plessy vs. Furgeson) A case involving Louisiana laws that required separate seating arrangements on busses and railroads. We have to fight like Jack Johnson, the great boxer who fought at Madison Square Garden, knowing that he would beat a White boxer every time. The next day in the south, there would be mass lynchings. This weighed heavy on Jack's thoughts, yet he pressed on for the betterment of the race. It was once said that that was the basis for King Kong! He wasn't hiding the fact that he loved White women. Ok, Ok, Just giving you a little history on him. The plight is still we have to fight. The biggest question I get is, who then do we fight? We fight ourselves first to rid our life of the bad habits and poisons of the system. Then we fight our community leaders to stay on a positive and righteous path. Next, the lawmakers and politicians that keep us in economical, physical, and educational bondage. Let us not forget We have discovered, in my opinion, seventy percent of the inventions on this planet. Facts! Thomas Edison, Alexander Graham Bell were all thieves! Edison had a sweatshop of African inventors.

Where he would choose which project to pursue, getting all the credit that he loved. It made him both famous and rich! Still, his most damaging attribution was the fact that in 1850. Thomas Edison made a movie about some of his slaves eating watermelons. The slaves were smiling ear to ear! This movie was seen all around the world. Right after this, you saw more racist propaganda on postcards, magazines, etc. This created the stereotype of Blacks as dumb and stupid. Yet, we still fought. During slavery, we were the agricultural inventors. The slaves! We had to be creative. Why? Because being creative made our lives better. Remember, the Massa has always just sat on his ass! We had to come up with a solution as a people!

NEW BEGINNINGS

"When deeds speak, words are mean less."

African Proverb

After slavery's end, there were new beginnings on both sides. The slaves left from the south to discover America. Don't get me wrong, a lot stayed creating sharecropping and ultimately suffering thru peonage. These two White supremacist economical systems created a new day for the Whites, while discovery created one for the Blacks. George Washington Carver invented the production line for Henry Ford. Carver studied plants creating the mass production line off the food production line in plants. The military came and recruited him for the plant's invention, which is when he discovered soybean. Some say he warned them that I was not good to eat yet. They ignored him. That is why we have a real spike in cancer. The sad thing it was a Black inventor's discovery, and we as Blacks are dying from the soybean-made food that they are feeding us daily. Don't believe me check the cancer rates and dates. Now take, for instance, Patterson. Patterson was a slave in West Virginia. He escaped and fled to Ohio, later starting a horse-and-drawn carriage company. This slave's ambition would lead him to construct the first Black-owned luxury car company.

In 1915 he rolled out his first cars, still just like in the 1960s. When the African race cried for freedom, the White racist government cried for widespread abortion, trying to kill the babies of the revolutionist. The Whites at this time cast a plan also out of peonage and sharecropping with future billions of dollars soon to be made. First off, let me give you an idea of how these systems work. First sharecropping. The ex-slave owners let the ex-slaves stay on the land and cultivate it for a share of the profit. Pimping! Peonage was where if you didn't have working papers, they would arrest you for vagrancy. Then you would be sent to the coal mines, steel mines, and work camps owned by the judges, sheriff, and governor's friends.

Them all making free money off of your labor, Pausing for a second to point out this. This is horrifically similar to today's prison system. Especially in Georgia! Still, the free money created off these companies led to a new beginning for all White supremacists, also slave money! The biggest example of slave money would be Joel Hunt. He was a known plantation owner, racist, and slaver. He beat his slaves without hesitation. Hunt would punish his slaves in the cruelest of fashions. He was quoted to have said, "I believe slaves in my coal mines could never be whipped too much." In 1893 he took his hard-earned slave money and bought a streetcar company. As time went on and business evolved. The company becomes Georgia power! This wealth didn't stop! Joel Hunt's younger brother Ernest Woodruff brought Coca-Cola in 1919 for 25 million of the families' hard-earned slave money. Next was Chattahoochee Brick company owner James Wenglish. He was also a known slave owner. His daughter married a bank executive named James Robinson. Mr. Wenglish gave the son-in-law piles of his slave money to start the fourth national Bank. This bank grew staggeringly, and in 1985 it was purchased and renamed Wachovia. The irony in that is staggering. Picture hundreds of millions made of slaves invested in buying a bank. These new-age hundreds of millions of economical slavery get taxed by these same banks adding more capital to the slave owner's bloodline. This is crazy! Still again, this is chess, not checkers.

Last but not least, the big boys Rockefeller and Carnegie, which we all know their families, become rich off the companies built off slavery money. Our government has profited alongside these criminals because they are criminals also. Jim Waters Homes in 1969 acquired Sloss Sheffield Iron and steel company. This company had the longest-running recorded history of operating slaves and slave ran mines in Alabama. They made millions off of slave labor. Still, our government made deals with them, creating economically disadvantaged housing programs. Still, they made money off the ancestors of the slaves they had beaten, broken, and worked.

Fredric Bastiat once said, "When plunder becomes a way of life for a group of men living together in society, they create for themselves in the time a legal system tha authorizes it, and a moral code tha glorifies it." That is exactly the problem with the united states; we must realize that these bankers and politicians are aligned and looking out for their future bloodlines. They install policies and laws to just do such. In 2020 President Joe Biden promised the Black public change and relief of a systemic system of police brutality. Upon gaining his presidency, he signed a bill classifying hate crimes against Asians because of COVID-19 backlash to be federal. The Black in America had been fighting for an anti-African American bill in this country for decades, yet again we were using and manipulated to help a cause that no longer needed us.

In this chapter, I wanted to give you a flashback and a trip throughout the history of our struggles and some triumphs. I choose these topics to reveal to the readers the different tricks and tactics placed in this system. That still strongly exists today! These old systems of peonage, sharecropping, population control and controlling our migration and progress are real. I wanted readers to understand the severity of their tricks, systems, and future plots.

CHAPTER 8

FREEDOM FIGHTERS

THE DESIRABLES

"Your philosophy determines your thought pattern, your thought pattern determines your attitude, your attitude determines your behavior pattern, and your behavior pattern determines your action."

Anthony T. Browder

After the American-born Africans went thru hell to get freedom from the bondage of slavery. They now had hidden challenges that haunted them from every aspect of life, yet you had some Blacks that still lead the way! Slavery didn't die with the 13th amendment in 1865. Slavery, the great beast, was only injured. The beast reemerged stronger thru White supremacy! For the readers that know a little history, you should know that race is just as much a part of this nation's history as the stars and stripes on the flag. Our nation was built on slavery, and this fact will never change. Slaveries fire only toned down; it reemerged as convict leasing laws, Jim Crow laws, now the new slavery prison! To most, slavery didn't end until the voting rights act, which was passed in 1965. Yes, the one drop of blood system, the three-fifths clause, all these racist tools would work well until 1965. The voting rights act divorced the race card and other issues with the right to vote, yet still, you have issues.

In 2018 the election, you had voter fraud and isolation from the polls for African Americans. That was heavily televised. In my opinion, the one thing that Black people should have learned from our great racist president George Washington was to take what you need. Yes, our first president taught me a valuable lesson. Not verbally, but by watching his movements. Fact! George Washington didn't have wooden teeth. He had the teeth of some of his slaves. Sized and yanked out and made into dentures. These same dentures are on display at his museums. That's taking what you need! The great Jamil Abdulah Al Amin, aka H-Rap Brown, once said, "Racism systemically verifies itself anytime the slave says we can only be free by Imitating his master." After reconstruction to prove we as free Black were special, the new Negro movement was pivotal. Its core value meant that Blacks were to be educated, in the arts, music and literature refined, an intellectual, almost Victorian. They were politically respectfully clean-cut, the reverse of being nasty and uneducated. This new Negro movement was to combat a critical era in our history.

At this time, the minstrel shows we regaining popularity. These were the Black face shows, where performers had Black painted faces, with big painted on red lips. (The Sambo). The new refined Negro movement fought back against that stereotype and ultimately showed that the Blacks were not uneducated and savage. This is around the time that the first Black graduate of Harvard, the great Mr. W.E.B. Dubois, came onto the scene. He was critical to the new Negro movement. He helped educate the culture and fought the uneducated stereotype by not being what they said we were. When fighting a war, you have different battles. Let's say during the war against African enslavement/oppression. From my perspective, we have had three major wars/battles against these racist systems in our history. Let's say the first resistance was fought in Africa with Shaka, Nazinga etc. The second resistance came when the slaves hit the slave lands of America, the islanders' revolts, Nat turner, Tousant, etc. This time now, in this

Break the Chains

section/chapter, in my opinion, would be considered the third great war. This era of 1960-1980. This is where Blacks were proud to be Black. Blackness was greatness, yet still shown no negativity around the world. We still held a fist to the sky, yelling, "I am Black and I am proud!" This third resistance was pivotal in our survival. The age of Malcolm, Martin and the Panthers felt like the age of African American Intellectualism. This time in history, we as a race were ready to die for equality. This scared America, yet if we would have only saw the economic effects of our movements. The Montgomery boycott and others. This would have killed the White supremacist capitalism at heart. This affected their money! They were most afraid when the Panthers taught banking, taxes, etc. They feared when Marcus Garvey taught self-dependence to the Blackman or Malcolm spoke of religious independence. Why? Because if we only made a stand, we would have crippled the system. Africans are the biggest race in the world. How can we be the minority economically or mentally? Che Guevara said, "In revolution, one wins, and one dies." There has to be a risk to receive the reward. Painstakingly as it is to accept, Martin, Malcolm, Medgar, etc., had to be martyrs for our liberation in the Revolution." When we started our propaganda toward this end. Several of our so-called intellectual Negro's who have been bamboozling the race for over half a century said we were crazy. That the Negro people of the western world were not interested in Africa. "This is crazy! This is reverse propaganda. The quote above by Mr. Marcus Garvey was correct because, at the same time, they were still interested in Africa for oil, diamonds, Gold etc. Mr. Garvey stated this to show how blind the African American Negro was. They told us Africa was worthless; they tried to teach us it was savage land jungle. While they plundered, stole, and oppressed, the rest of the Africans there. The sad part is most Black Americans listened and didn't care about Africa or their lost bloodline's welfare. One of the pivotal leaders of this movement, in my eyes, was Marcus Garvey. Marcus Garvey was born in Jamaica in 1887.

In August 1920, Mr. Garvey in Black attire and a headdress lined with features marched thousands of Blacks down Lenox Ave in New York. Mr. Huch Mulzac of Garvey's (Black Star Navy) recalled that day. "It was as The Greatest demonstration of colored solidarity in American history Before or since!" During this time, there became a divide in the race; you had the Blacks who wanted integration, and some like Garvey called out for separation. Garvey once was quoted to say. "W.E.B. Dubois represented the antebellum Negro whose time was fast running out. He had obligated himself to the White folks."

Garvey believed in Black Independence; he was planning on organizing a Black bank. He knew we had to pool our money together like the Europeans had done to oppress us to win. We had to have economic independence to get their attention. In my opinion, The Montgomery Bus Boycott was the biggest example of Black economic empowerment in the USA. It showed the Whites that they had to listen. They lost jobs, money, and businesses lost money; it disabled that town completely economically. That taught us to get the money first! Then they have no choice but to listen. All we have to do even today is Boycott to show our economic power! So, I ask why? Why won't we go against the system that plans to incarcerate us for drugs? They want us to have six different kids with different women and don't raise them. They don't want us to be fathers, mothers, brothers, and sons. Assatta Shakur said, "If we are deaf, dumb, and blind to what's happening in the world, your under no obligations to do anything, but if you know what's happening, and you don't do anything, but sit on your ass, then your nothing but a punk!"

Blacks started to pick sides! The movement they started was pivotal. And most have forgotten the pride, greatness, and respect they called for. We as parents have forgotten to install loyalty, strength, and good character in our children. Most importantly, we have to set great examples first! If not, then we will get bullshit mentality's in our kids. We have to install the good seed in our children first, then water it with good ideas and morals. Malcolm X's father was a (UNIA) Division President. Malcolm's parents even meet at a (UNIA) Convention in Toronto, Canada. Both were devoted Garvey followers. That was the seed that showed Malcolm pride, respect, etc. Then life in the streets changed him to be a street person. Those trials & tribulations took him back to his roots as a leader and a better man, without that first instillation of good morals from his parents. The seed would have never grown!

Medgers Ever once said, "If I had to die for something, let it be the truth." This is the mentality we all should have. We should think as sister Souljah who said, "I am African first! I am Black First! I want what's good for me, my people first, and if my survival means your total destruction, then so be it. "We have to get back to understanding and accepting the pain that comes with liberation. We are dying by the thousand with police brutality, drugs, diseases, etc., yet to know we have future Martin's, Malcolm's, Medgar's, and Garvey's to fight against the system!

Painstakingly today, in 2021, it's not about a southern system of race or a United States system of race, but a global system of race. We as Africans, have to change the system altogether globally. We have to change the stereotype globally. Martin Luther King said, "He had never seen hate in the south as strong as he did in Chicago, Illinois. He said, "It was worse than even Mississippi." This shows that racism was not just a southern problem! During their movement in the '60s, '70s, and the '80s, the Blacks were relentless in fighting for equality. This Black Movement wore America out the force of these great men and women pushed America into a corner. The force of Elijah, Stokely, Malcolm, Martin etc., made America come with a different plan, a different smokes screen. They then devised a way to weaken the movement, to weaken the people. They hated for us to fight their oppression. The singer Billy Holiday and the story of the song "Strange Fruit." She was only being an artist, and like most artists, she used drugs. They stalked her, set her up and locked her up multiple times. All because the song was about lynching Blacks in the south. They even tried to plant drugs and handcuff her on her death bed. This is crazy! Our own government started to push more heroin, cocaine into the Black Communities. Why? This was done to weaken the struggle, to weaken the bloodline, to weaken the cause. They wanted to ensure that this new Black pride would end and never reemerge this evolution of Black psychology. The FBI, led by Mr. Hoover, developed at this time a Black Militant department. They did this to monitor the Black leaders and Detour other new Black leaders from emerging. They developed a plan for a new system that runs like a machine even today. This system uses drugs, money, and different economical tactics to profit and keep the system afloat. This new system is called prison!

THE UNDESIRABLES

Break the Chains

"The most dangerous of all dependence is to depend on your powerful oppressor to free you and share power with you because powerful people never train the powerless people to take their power away from them."

John Henrick Clarke

Just like you had the desirable people in the Black American revolution, you definitely have undesirable people. People that were infiltrators, spies, and snitches. People that lived to keep the movement down and going backward. The famous group Sly and The Family Stone said, "Dying young is hard to take but selling out is harder." This subsection talks about the sellouts, the uncle Toms, the Mami, coons, and compromisers of the African bloodline. There have always been compromisers helping kill off our race. Their own race! Since the first European boat landed in Africa. It's sad but true!

The U.S historically recorded that the first full-time Black federal officers were hired to infiltrate the Marcus Garvey movement. Why? Because this is the time when Blacks started to show resilience to the oppression of the United States economically. That was done by the Italian MOBS puppet J. Edgar Hoover. This is ironic because the federal government prays on Blacks in America still today with its racist policies. Even today, people don't know about the great sell-outs in African history. Today I will bring some of them to the light. First, I wanted to start with the compromiser and traitor R.R Morton. Mr. Morton was a US Army Officer of intelligence, and the government turned him into Booker T. Washington's school's vice principal. The government hired him to check if Mr. Washington was educating Blacks properly and not hiding Black revolutionaries. Sad but again true! Next, the sellout Eugene Roberts was probably one of the greatest compromisers of Black bigotry. He spied on Malcolm X., then after Malcolm was killed. He spied on the Black Panther movement until it was dismantled. The Blacks never figured him out. Still, throughout this, our movement thrived.

By the 1960' Black population control was almost a religion for White America. From the start, they made it clear that if you didn't play their game, they would cut you off financially. This scared the compromisers to the point they did whatever was asked. If that didn't work, they would kill you. We all know the stories of Martin, Malcolm, and Medgar Evers, but how many know the story of Samuel Yet. Samuel Yet was a US Air force veteran that served in the Korean war as the director of equal opportunity. He had a master's degree from Indiana University and was an award-winning journalist. In 1968, he was the first African American hired by News Week. He was their Washington D.C. correspondent. Mr. Yet wrote a book called "The Choice" This book was about the Black genocide through abortion. When the book came out, News Week fired him. In a meeting with his boss, Mr. Yet asked, "Why?" His boss told him that the call came down from the White House. Why would the White House staff no agree with the book? What secrets did it tell? Regardless of their schemes. The books still sold well, winning two national awards. Then mysteriously, his publisher took the book off the market. Again, trying to hide the knowledge. Mr. Yet had no help; he had no coalition to come to his aid.

Sadly, the one who sounded the alarm gets the least help and support from the righteous in today's time. The NAACP and other groups didn't aid

Mr. Yet in getting a fair fight for our rights, yet they left him to dry in the sun. Ishmael Hernandez, the Executive Director of the African Caribbean center, stated in 2003, "The civil rights elite had forgotten the lives of urban Black children and has joined those who chose to kill them." Unbelievable! They have forgotten that racists snatched Black babies from the mother's arms and sold them into slavery in the past! Today they snatched them from the mother's womb and threw them in the garbage. This is a true but horrible statement. One of the slyest compromisers in my book is the great Jessie Jackson.

In Jet Magazine, in 1975, Jackson called for a ban on abortion and stuck to his guns, calling abortion genocide for Black Americans. Then in 1981, he realized he needed funding from the democratic party and Planned Parenthood like corporations to run for president. He compromised his morals and people for monetary gain. He then stated that "abortion was a woman's choice." Before Roe vs. Wade, the first anti-abortion groups were the Black Panthers and The Nation of Islam. White supremacist groups and the higher-ups realized. Even the Black churches started to take notice. In 1972 at the national Black caucus Charles Digs stated that he did not trust the abortion industry and family help organizations. He kept this stance strongly until the money flowed in. When they realized they could get funding from these groups for not seeking against them. The majority flipped, just like Jesse Jackson, who once said, "What happens to the mind of a person and the moral fabric of a nation that accepts aborting the life of a baby without a ping of conscience? What kind of society will we have twenty years from now, hence if life can be taken so casually? "This is what Blacks of that time stood on. This is what they knew as facts. That abortion was geared to hurt us. In my opinion, every pro-choice Black politician is our greatest sellout. Point blank! Because with a little research, anyone can find out what is going on in this God-forsaken country. So, either they don't look or don't care!

The great Alveda King has been trying for years to bring this problem to the light. The fact that the NAACP is in bed with Planned Parenthood and has been now for years. She has held picket signs and yelled outside for hours in front of the great global hall, yet they hide this type of protest from the Black community in the media. Why? Because it would strengthen our people, educate our people. Marcus Garvey said, "We feel now just as the whole White race would feel if they were to be governed and ruled by the Chinese. If we lived in our own districts, let us rule those districts. If we have the majority in our communities, let us run those communities. We form a majority in Africa, and we naturally govern ourselves there. No man can govern another man's house as well as himself. Let us have fair play. Let us have justice." This is the appeal we make to White America. This is the place we call home, though. The united states, in my opinion, is a place full of smoke screens and lies. Not only the United States but other parts of the world also. In my point of view, even Gandhi was a racist. Gandhi wrote on March 7, 1908, "Kaffers (Blacks) are as a rule uncivilized, the convicts even more so. They are troublesome, very dirty and live almost like animals." Gandhi was referring to the Davidians. The descendants of Africans and Indians. Gandhi never gave these people support in his land. Why? He also never spoke up for the Blacks in South Africa going thru apartheid. Why? As Doctor Johnson asked, why is there a statue of him outside Martin Luther King's monument in Atlanta? Why? Because this was done to mislead the Blacks youth into believing that he was the reason for Martin's success. His ideology was the reason Martin was so powerful. When actually, it was the opposite way around. Truth be told, if it were not for Martin's intellect and plight, most of the world would not have been so quick to listen to Gandhi. It's funny that the racist Charles Darwin Wrote. "It is not the strongest of species that survive nor the most intelligent, but the one most responsive to change." That's funny because we as a race have been captured, sold, released, and tricked for years in a racist system. Yeah, as the African race, I think we have been the ones most responsive to change! Black Moses stated, "We are being camouflaged, not so much by those with whom we are competing for our economic, political existence but by men from within our own race, either as agents of the opposition, or just an unconscious fools who are endearing to flatter us into believing that our future should rest on chance. Blacks have depended for far too long on a system that wants us to fail or people that want us to fail. During the Black empowerment movement, the Klu Klux Klan reappeared and flexed its muscles as a powerful terrorist organization by killing people bombing homes, churches even castrating Blacks. Why did they reemerge? Because they felt the fear of the Black Panthers, NAACP, and other Black righteous organizations in the '60s, '70s, and '80s. They have now realized that their agenda and the governments are one we see that with Donald Trump and his clan friends and supporters. Still, today they sit back and let us kill each other with drugs, guns, HIV, and a host of other on purpose, well-placed traps! As Black, we should be aware of these traps and be aware that sometimes our own people set them! Compromisers!

CHAPTER 9

NEW DAY

THE WHITE MAN'S NEW TRICK

In 1970 Martin Luther King Jr. said, "If the conditions do not change soon in America, This country will have a Fascist Police State." When I see what's going on in 2020, this is what we are experiencing now! The militarization of America's police forces was not a mistake. It was done intentionally by Presidents Nixon, Regan, and Clinton. All to incarcerate Black men. My thoughts on today's treatment of African Americans by law enforcement are. This was inevitable because we have shown many of the phenomena to many glitches in the Willie Lynch Theory. Which states when this phenomenon is found, it has to be reminded, forces to remember, and put back in line! With excessive force on strictly on Blacks by law enforcement! Wow!

The vast depths of deception the oppressors have taken to derail African Americans is unimaginable! I've sat back for years and watched African Americans poison themselves mentally, physically, and socially. The whole world has watched as Black Americans became the victims of police brutality, voter registration discrimination, and a host of politically corrupted agendas, all designed to hold us back! The world watched as the United States Judicial system bent laws to incriminate and monetize the judicial system against Blacks through mandatory minimums, three-strikes laws, and bias stand your ground laws. Simultaneously they did this while still devastating the family structure with drugs, alcohol, and diseases. They put harmful chemicals in our food, causing cancer, high blood pressure, diabetes, etc. All these things were meant to break the African Americans to destroy his rise to power and greatness. These things were done to stagnate our growth. They didn't plan on all those things building us, molding us, making us stronger and more powerful!

Doing time in prison taught me respect, independence, self-worth, and patience. The latter one is the most valuable lesson anyone could learn. The Swahili word for patience is Sabali. My grandmother told me this in the parking lot in 2010 before turning myself into Fulton County Jail. She looked at me with tears in her eyes and said, " Chino, just be patient, and baby, everything will get clear with time. Just concentrate on your new life when this is all over." My grandmother died in 2015 before getting out and ever telling her how correct she was. I learned in prison that life is challenging and that you have to do the work to become greater. To change, you have to want to fix your situation. So, I had patience and put in the work and learned. One of the things I learned just by watching was that it is far easier to put a puzzle together from the outside in than inside out. Starting with all the corners and edges first, then working your way into the middle slowly, binging the picture into focus. Ultimately completing the puzzle. Symbolically I felt we should apply this to our lives; we have to fix the outside first. Your friends, family, etc. Then ultimately you. Then you will start to see the picture that your surroundings are creating for you! We have to do this with ourselves, community, and family to break the chains of the negative stereotype and thoughts.

On April 10, 2010. I woke up around 3:00 am, made coffee, and started my day, as usual, watching the news. I normally watched about an hour of it before I started to study or write. What I saw that morning was so disturbing. It had me literally ready to fight anyone. The news headlines read in bold letters. "INVASION" They spoke of the Mexicans fleeing oppression and violence in South America, rushing the American border. They said 900 or more children were misplaced without their parents. This reminded me of the African slave trade. They showed the children in dog cages. I thought of the Indians first, then the Africans all being treated the same way. They separated and treated them like animals also. This hurt me deeply; it reminded me of how devious, selfish, and unhuman. The great United States is. They don't care about humanity. In the grand scheme of the pursuit to control the world, humanity and humility mean nothing.

Still, the biggest question I had was. How were the descendants of the first American inhabitants the Indian Invading anyway? Where their people not here first! This reminded me of the story of archaeologist Carl Malx. Carl Malx looked for years to find a European discovery in Africa that would prove they were there first. When he found a Zimbaee ruin of Mapungupoy, it contained gold artifices. He claimed that Africans couldn't have made these artifacts or this structure. He was convinced that Whites had done it. It's funny that the Dutch setters wanted to claim the excavation under the pretense they arrived first. It was later discovered through technology that the Africans had been there for thousands of years before the Duch even came to Africa. It baffles me tremendously, like how could you even think that you were there first when your people traveled to get there and the Africans were there.

Let me ask you, the reader, a question if you don't mind. Why does the new immigration bill not include most African countries, Haiti included. How are Cubans and most European nations allowed in, but no Blacks? Because in the oppressor's eyes, the Mexican has replaced the Africans in the United States economical workforce. They don't need any new Africans! They have been trying to get rid of the old ones. They have been trying to do this since 1865 with the 1st amendment. They don't want us here. Still, we believe we are equal in their minds. W.E.B. Dubois said," I was walking in a town and looked inside at store and saw a sign that read. Sam Hoses Knuckles. It was actual knuckles of a Black man who had been lynched in that town and dismembered. The savages had his knuckles on display like a trophy. Still, they called us savages! They have always despised us; they have always tried to prolong our progress. So, I ask. Who do we look to for our help? "The pro-choice politicians, or the preachers that accept hundreds of thousands of their money to keep you decile. The bush family took a page out of how to break a slave, and Margret Singer notes and killed off the Black church from being a pillar in the community simply by setting guidelines for their faith-based funding. I ask you, the reader. How when their own laws state, there is a strict separation of government and state. Still, they use these laws for their own betterment and our pain.

America was built off of capitalism. An in a capitalistic government, you have to make or have a large pool of workers and poor to get rich off of. So they do all they can to keep us poor, working for them, and government dependent. With smokescreens such as high-interest bank loans and aftermarket debit cards, check cashing stations, denial of small business loans etc.

An Arab Indian and I had a conversation one day, and he said, He and his friends laughed at African Americans because we have been here for 500 years and have gained nothing. I knew he was not a racist but just blind to our plight. I then explained that most Blacks are kept from financial knowledge and stability. Because with that, the Blacks would hurt the system. I explained that if half The Black people in the United States got a business loan they applied for, foreigners receive. It would cripple the system. Why? Because we then would do as they do and hire our own. Then they wouldn't have workers. I explained to him the pains of our struggle and the numerous martyrs we have had. He revealed he had no idea about a lot of the things I said. He then apologized and said that we were the strongest race on earth. We talked business for a second; then I explained that. It is a well-known fact that most wealthy European corporations do not mix or deal with African lead corporations. Again, that would be giving us help. Help that we don't receive, that they as foreigners do with tax breaks, etc. He smiled and understood. He understood because, without money, we cannot progress also. We have to economically get our lives and community together.

The great Marcus Garvey knew this and the great Gadhafi was murdered because of this. He and the other African States were about to construct Africa's first Central Bank. They were going to bank Africa's money on their sources in the ground of Africa. This would have killed the global economic order in the world. It would have Instantly killed the US dollar, pound, yen, and Euro. Why because Africa has the biggest natural resource reserve in the world. This would have made Africa a superpower. Thus, killing the neo-colonialism in Africa. The world bank and other power organizations didn't want that. The big companies that feed off of African's and Africa people still today didn't want that!

NEW SLAVERY

Break the Chains

"It is not enough to understand, you must have the power of realization."

RaUnnefer Ameen

It's baffling fact to me that five percent of the world's population live in the United States, yet we have a twenty-five percent incarceration rate. The highest in the world. The stats say that In 1972 there were 300,000 Blacks incarcerated. By the year 2021, there are 2.3 million. I ask you, the reader, what happened what changed. More baffling is that one in three of those incarcerated is African American. I once read in a book that Senator Daniel Patrick Moynihan said, "Basically after the Civil Rights time died, America made all the promises to Black leaders speaking about equality etc., lying." They realized that if they promise nothing, we expected nothing. When the government refuses to effect reform and implement justice, the people lose respect for the institution of the government. Over two-thirds of this world population consist of people of color. Crime stats for African Americans have always been high, and they will never decrease to appease the public because the system is not designed that way. The restriction on Blacks has always been greater. Even today, with the racist laws, like stop and frisk, driving while Black etc. Historically the White House set the president in the USA for racial equality. Once, people saw that Barack Obama had no intentions in the Trayvon Martin case. In my opinion, a mental green light was sounded in the USA. And we as Black Americans sat by and watched a spike in televised Black killings, and most did nothing. Obama was a puppet! African Americans believed in him and behind the scene, he let us down and sold us out. Under the Obama administration Black unemployment rate the incarceration rate was higher than the last three presidents. Why? Why did the Latin Community give President Obama millions of dollars in contributions? Why because? That employs him to listen to them. Politically speaking, the word minority to a Latino politician is a way of saying they want the benefits of the Black American Civil Rights movement, yet they don't want to identify with being Black or having African Blood. Crazy but true!

All of these things help deprive the American Black. Help to stagnate him. In 1990 the KKK announced that it has intended to join the battle against illegal drugs. By becoming the eyes and ears of the police. This is not the first time they helped rid the nation of African Americans. After the highly racial and controversial movie The Birth of a Nation. The KKK played a bigger role in policing African Americans. This resulted in mass lynchings all across America. Still, nothing was done. Why? Because they now are policing Blacks with the police and the undercover Klansman /police brothers. During the Clinton term in Washington, Clinton slashed funding for public housing by $7 billion, a reduction of 61%, and boosted corrections constructions of prisons. This is crazy; they are prepping our children for Prison! The Clinton administration also increased federal and state prison numbers higher than any president. This was all done to make money! The Presidents have never been on the Black side of America! From the Founding fathers to President Obama. We have forgotten that in 1992 bill Clinton let Ricky Ray Rector die. Ricky was a mentally retarded Blackman who had so little conception of what was about to happen to him That he asked for dessert from his last meal to be saved for the next day! The man thought he wasn't going to die!

Break the Chains

Have we forgotten the Willie Horton ad, which featured a dark-skinned Blackman, a convicted murderer who escaped while on work furlough, and he raped and murdered a White woman at home? Bush Sr. did this. This is the same propaganda they used to promote slavery. They kill us without impunity! Have we forgotten Kalif Browder, who killed himself after suffering the horrors of the game to capture Black men? The youngest person ever executed was George Junius Stinney Jr., a 14-year-old. He was falsely accused of killing two White girls in Colombia, SC. They convicted him with no evidence. Nothing to say; this child did this grown man crime. The United States prison system is the New Slavery. The government makes millions off of Blacks incarcerations. A more alarming fact is that Private Companies now make billions off the same game, and no one says anything. Is this all planned, or is this just how it is?

In 1968 President Nixon's right-hand man was recorded saying what most White politicians at that time were thinking. He stated that America had two enemies at the time. One was the anti-war left (Hippies), and the other was the African American. He stated that the government couldn't exterminate or incarcerate either legally but by getting the public to associate the hippies with marijuana and the Blacks with heroin. Thus, making them look criminal, then they could disrupt communities, arrest leaders, and vilify them both on the news. During the Regan era, the Negative propaganda against African Americans reached new heights. He publicly screamed it was a war on drugs; secretly, this was a war on Black America. With the aid of groups like A.L.E.C and others who have planned, plotted, and executed their plans against African Americans with the aid of our government and a legal system that has a 97% plea bargain rate and the high incarceration rate on African Americans. I ask what is next? We need more humanization and love than incarceration and hate first. Then we can begin to heal and move forward.

CHAPTER 10
CHAINS

PLACING (CAUSE)

"Never interrupt your enemy when he is making a mistake!"

JOHN MILTON

During slavery, there were not just physical chains placed on the newly inducted Americans, called slaves. There were deeper mental chains. Chains that held mental restrictions, diseases, and fears. Fears that remain close to the Black American phycology today. The American slave was openly breaded to be a brainless feeble-minded, and docile being. They understood that the knowledge and history they withheld from us was withholding us from being us! The American slaves were again mistreated again like no other. He was prevented from education, his bloodline, his culture, and his true religion. Knowing that the bloodline was cut poses a tremendous threat and responsibility to the Black man. He now has to find himself in culture, present time, and history. This was a tremendous part in the placing of the chains of slavery. I ask you, what do you think are the effects of just one phycological part of the chains of slavery? Most of Black Americas, educational housing, mental health, health, family structural problems come from the effects of slavery. If they are not directly, but in the span of time, slavery's causes lead to the 1960s, '70s, and 2000s effects of the Black race. The feeling that an African American man has in his mind as a child that he has to start from nothing. Comes from slavery! The struggles you go thru in life with educational bias. Even racial profiling when you try to relax at the mall, restaurants, and theatres comes from -

slavery.

How could people not understand that? If you have a traumatic event in your life, this event renders certain natural reactions to anything involving the event. This also happens when similar actions or causes for the event that happens around the individual. Strangely this mental awareness happens in all species on this planet. It's evolution or simply learning? Take for instance, the way zebras understand that alligators wait in the water or how the child will most likely repeat a Parent drug use. Human beings' developmental environments are detrimental to the psychological mindset of the person. As stated in the Willie Lynch letter, the system broke the man and repositioned the woman but left an imprint on the mentality of the Black American youth. This they also knew. Yet, they continued because it helped their agenda. They wanted us to make fatherless children because they will soon get frustrated with minimal public-school educations, and most will quit seeking knowledge or education. They most likely will start a life of crime, then go to prison! Making them even richer. Most don't understand the pride of being descendants of Kings and Dynasties. The little knowledge that Black Americans are taught of our history is a smokescreen, and the real history Is so precious that most don't understand its importance. Today's generational lack of knowledge reminds me of when. The Arabians enriched and expanded their culture by copying the most important literature they could find. The best literature had been destroyed mostly during the dark ages. Yet, most of the African literature had been destroyed. Some works made it like Mohammed Kati, Rahmanes, Sadian ashamed a bass made it. There was no one to pick up the mantle. What's sad about this is that most Blacks don't even understand the age or worth of their works,

Break the Chains

just our bloodline, education, and knowledge. They are all priceless!

Still, we have Africans that have been looking for acceptance since we got off the boat. We gave up our names, religion, and culture, trying to be accepted by a European society. Not knowing this acceptance will never happen. The great Ayi Kwei Armah said, "Endless our struggle must seem to those whose vision reaches only to the end of today.

Slavery was and still is today a taboo subject. Why? Racism is so restricted that most people don't talk about it. But how can we change without discussing the subject first? Let me give you a similar scenario. Say, "We African Americans symbolically were a molested child, and we are crying about being molested years ago. No human would say, "Oh, that was so long ago, stop crying about it, get over it!" NO! What we would do is help seek justice for that child. So why is it that no one seeks justice for African Americans? Justice Socially, mentally, and financially. How do we not get extra tax breaks or housing breaks in good neighborhoods? How is it that a people who gave everything building this great nation? Be last financially yet first in health-related deaths, incarceration, unemployment etc. Why as Ralph Waldo Ellison said, "It takes a deep commitment to change and even deeper commitment to grow." The cultural chains that White supremacy promoted, we still deal with today. The world believed as they promoted Africa as a savage land, and the people believed we as Africans naturally were savage people. They never promoted Africa as one of God's gifts to mankind and one of the most beautiful places on earth. They always showed Africa as a jungle, swamps, or badlands, yet it is more jungle in Europe and Asia than it is in Africa! Americans were always showing the poor hunter-gatherer Africans. They never showed or praised the queens and kings or great people like Mana Musa and Shaka Zulu. This placement of negative images to the world was not done mistakenly. Some may say it was just a part of them showing African culture to the world. Why didn't we see the good parts, the kings and queens, etc.? Yet they showed us naked with bones in noses and boiling pots like we were cannibals and savages. Thus, creating a race of Europeans that think the same way, even to this day in the European culture. How many have seen the Sami tribe? Some of you don't even know who I'm speaking of. The Sami tribe was an original Caucasian tribe that was Hunter-Gatherers. They were also naked and savage for centuries, yet we never see them. Why? Because it would show them before they were Victorian, civilized, and before the dark ages. Which honestly Africans helped them do with soap and other natural products of hygiene. Still, as Africans, we try to mock them, to emulate them. Why? When they have always mocked and tried to emulate us. In music, art, fashion, etc. For centuries, philosophers have known that what trips up the slave is the desire to gain recognition from the master. We keep trying to persuade White people to recognize and acknowledge our worth as a people and race. For what, I ask? We are trying to impress the wrong people when we need to impress ourselves.

One of the functions of this slave trading, demoralizing and restructuring machine called the United States. It was to break down the Black family systematically in every generation. Why? It's simple because they understood that the family was the strongest unit of social cohesion and resistance to slavery in simpler terms for Africans. They understood by destroying your family, bloodline and taking your culture. This systematically destroys every generation. These mental chains were the best way to ensure a perpetual existence of an abject underclass. Whose labor and upkeep would remain as cheap as possible. Now we, as Blacks in America, struggle with gentrification in the inner city. This pool of badness creating a platform for gang activity and drug use.

Just as it did in Africa with apartheid, I honestly believe that this deep African importance is important during slavery in New Orleans. This lead to a deep-rooted African Indian culture in New Orleans. This hate for our survival and culture has been a thorn in the United States side for a long time. The US government has been trying to kill the Africans for a long time. Katrina was no surprise; New Orleans has long been a bad place for Blacks in America. A problem, issues after slavery. Let's not get it confused 1861 was only 150-160 years ago. Most of the main participants just died and their kids are definitely in positions of power and grandkids. These White supremacists definitely carry on the same traits as their grandfathers. The same way Blacks do. We both carry the pains of slavery. This is very true, yet the Black man has lost so much that his life is his pain.

Even today, New Orleans is still a thorn in the United States side. Most don't notice the chains. Take, for instance, the world's issue with slavery that gets less attention than the Trump prostitute scandal. This is very true but sad during the Haitian earthquake crisis Prime Minister of Haiti. Mr. Jean May Bellderive stated, "After the earthquake, the Europeans came in and we're organ harvesting and kidnapping children for child sex slaves. This is unbelievable! Huh? Still, the Americans didn't help. Strangely at least 25,000 Black people go missing without a trace in the United States a year. It is highly believed they, too are being either sex trafficked or organ harvested. There have been multiple cases in my state of Georgia. A young male Kendrick Johnson drop-dead mysteriously and later, when he was exhumed for the belief of foul play, no organs were found in his body. Mr. Johnson wasn't an organ donor, so where were his organs? This is crazy; they once stole your children for slavery, then stole them out of their mother's womb for disposal. Now when they die they, steal their organs. Still, we see this and don't fight! We see it and don't understand that in two days, two years, five years, this could be your child, your sister, aunt, mother, or father. So why wait until it's too late? We have to first understand that the invisible chains of hatred upon them are stronger than the ones in ourselves, our culture, and our community. This is a far greater disease than HIV, or cancer, a disease that will keep carrying on if left unchecked until the Black man is no more!

REMOVAL (EFFECT)

"We are the ones we've been waiting for."

June Jordan

The greatest African American revolutionist that set foot in the United States. "In My Opinion," Mr. Marcus Garvey said, "The African male is no there for fun or play or to entertain the European world!" "The African hasn't survived the centuries of hardship and difficulties, Just to die again." In my opinion, die again through gangs, drugs, prostitution, AIDS, alcoholism, etc. Garvey said, "He naturally must have been learning by experience, and that experience ought to guide him over the shoals of twentieth century's political bankruptcy." Have you the Black male or female, never question your greatness, your morality? Have you ever asked yourself if the African is inferior, why would the elitist do so much to hold him down? Why try so hard to suppress his gifts, talents, and innovations to help mankind's advancement. Why imprison him with laws unequally made? Why? Let me tell you why, because if we were left alone. It would be the opposite of what they promoted, by us being dependent on them. We would thrive, change, and show our greatness. Greatness that helps not only to build America but the world!

Blacks helped fund most of the biggest cities and America and were detrimental in forging the existing ones. They brought in thousands in chains. In cities like Atlanta, Detroit, New York, New Orleans and so forth, the list goes on and on. Did we forget, the city of Los Angeles was founded by fourteen people in 1781? There were two Europeans; the rest were African and Indian. The Black descendants of Indians even founded Chicago. Beverly Hills was owned by Maria Zita Valdez, the granddaughter of a slave and Indian. Africans have done tremendous things in this country, and for what reward? A second-rate education, mass incarceration, a political and economic system designed to keep us in the projects and ghettos. In 1973, John Blossom game in (echoing heliconist) said, "The most remarkable aspect of the whole process of enslavement is the extent to which the American born slaves were able to retain their ancestor's culture." Still, how strange it is that we are so underdeveloped mentally, financially, and socially. Blacks have been scarred mentally. It would take a class at the best psychological studies college years to put them all down in so many ways. Financial effects are the same! It's amazing that we as Black Americans act as if we don't want financial freedom. We act as if we are scared of banks' stocks, investing in the future. It puzzled me at first! Then I did a little research to see why? My thoughts on this are basic because of years of mental games, slavery, and fear of a White supremacist system. Their tricks like the Freedman's Bank or Black Wall Street have left scars also. Black Americans simply feel that with a bank account, the European can just come and take everything. Then imprison you! There have been numerous Rich Black Americans that the system has brought upon bogus charges. Then bankrupted them. Maybe this is the reason that most Blacks don't save. Just spend! Well, that reason and a very shallow realization of financial education also. Then you have examples of Blacks that save, save, save, and the government still finds ways to come seize your assets. One example is the story of Yahweh Ben Yahweh. He was a Miami millionaire who was actually helping people in this country by creating better opportunities. He was worth almost a billion dollars. The government came with some trumped-up charges, didn't imprison him, but took all his assets. How? The better question is, Why? They knew that without capital, he couldn't help the communities that they wanted to see stagnant. They wanted the Blacks to be poor and dependent on the government. I guess delivering us from poverty is a crime in their eyes.

Have you ever asked yourself, Why does the media show young Black children's faces when they get arrested? The same news channel won't show White ones when they are getting arrested? Why? Because they want to keep promoting a criminal, thug, vagrant image, etc. If a White or Black child is watching this, he or she will get the idea that Black people are criminals in the world. They will think that in Africa, all the children are starving Ethiopians. TV portrays Africans in a horrible image. This fear will never change!

The southern stand your ground law is racist! Why? This law has repeatedly been shown to only work for Whites. If you are Black, there is no self-defense! Black America has to change so much that the majority will say. It's too much, and it's too hard. How? Most don't understand that the White supremacist elite has put these roadblocks in your path, just to make you say that. It's baffling that we let Black US politicians walk around like they're actually are accomplishing something. Don't get me wrong, you have some that do, yet to most, it's a paycheck versus public service. Sadly, they have always used Blacks to control, trick, and inform on other Blacks. This has been going on before American slavery or snitching, as we have named it. During slavery time, the Africans called them Compromisers.

After slavery, the divide was so distant Blacks again started to pick sides. You even had organizations like the blue vein society, where you couldn't join unless you could see your veins through your skin! The light-skinned Blacks were pitted against the dark-skinned Blacks. The effects we still see today! Why is it that Blacks don't understand that a diamond is still a diamond with flaws and imperfections included? The great Ra Unnefer Ameen once said, "It's not enough to understand; you must have the power of realization." And we haven't realized that we are greatness. We are the majority! Have you ever asked yourself why we, as African American parents tend to downplay our children's knowledge and talents? One reason being, because in slavery days, the mother didn't want the master to take notice of their children. This would mean being sold for the boys or raped for the girls. So, they didn't boast or encourage that kind of love and ambition in their kids. Sadly, this has been passed down also. Take for instance, the Sun Down Rule. It was said that Black people couldn't go to certain cities and be caught after the streetlights came on. This is where

Black mothers get the idea of having their family in before the streetlights come on. It was a book written by James Loral called "Sundown Towns." Have you ever asked yourself why the African woman has always been promoted in two ways: the hussy and Miami? The Miami image was a good, subservient, and a fearful subject to the master. All cuddly with the White children loving, yet toward her own, she was stern aggressive. She also was the same way toward the Black man in the house. Controlling the Black man, as Willie Lynch stated, The hussy image was promoted strictly for the White man's benefit because he wanted to feel good about raping the Black woman. Mentally he told himself it was her fault; she wanted it. One report in a medical journal said, "African women were naturally promiscuous because of their protruding buttocks and genitals. It's crazy because the 45% of White women who get buttock operations in 2020 must be promiscuous also, or maybe it was just what A. W. Calhoun said, "The fact that White men were raised by Mamy's, maybe that's why they were so infatuated with Black women." If so, that would explain why our great President Benjamin Franklin loved Black women. Him and a large part of the slave controlling racist rapist that defiled our Black women during slavery. Sad but true!

The Black man has long been a troublesome presence in the world, from our homelands of Africa to the slave coast of the United States. We have been beaten, under-spoken for, and misguided by the slavers and our own. It's amazing, we made it this far. Herbert Gutman said in his book, "The Black Family in Slavery and Freedom,"

In 1926, "We were a preserving people." He challenged the prevailing belief that slavery weakened and even destroyed the African Family in this country. He argued that the Black Family survived slavery with impressive strength. Bravely with this impressive strength came scars, mental ones that we cannot see. For instance, a Black man in Atlanta said he was so tired of getting racially profiled and harassed by police. That he finally shot one White officer. The pressure is so enormous that most don't believe it even exists. But I am here to tell you it's real! The story of Oda Banga saddens me every time I see an animal in the Zoo. Why? Because Oda was the 22-year-old African placed in a cage beside a gorilla in New York under Darwin's theory. This broken soul killed himself ten years later. This event was horrifying on the mindset of him and also America. This is very tragic still; we have the opposite.

Also, people like Fredrick Douglas, who around the same time was a prominent African American, were born in Maryland into slavery. He escaped in 1838, going north. Douglas quickly became the leader of the abolitionist movement. These are the ones that scared White America. The Malcolm's, Fedricks, Martins, and Marcus. In still, the reality of the situation is this. If the Black male is coerced to be a genetic threat, then the White man will never stop attacking him. It may not be direct, but his indirect approach is the worst. The mass incarceration, unemployment, minimal schooling, mass abortions, etc., will only eat us alive! These tricks and roadblocks only have forged the Black American into a force he doesn't even understand he possesses. The intuitiveness, adaptiveness, and natural skill set. It would surely make him a ruling class if only he realized it !!!

CHAPTER 11
SOLUTIONS

<u>MAN</u>

The webster definition for solution is simple.

An answer to a problem!

Today in America, we as African American men have to find an internal solution first. Then we may attempt to help heal the African woman from her mental scars also. Manning Marbele said it best, "I am convinced that the Black man will only reach his full potential when he learns to draw upon the strengths and insight of the back woman." This I totally agree with. like the old saying goes. "Behind every strong Black man, there is a strong Black woman." First, we, as Black men, have to be leaders and real men. This will then give the African American female something worth choosing. Then the women will follow! We as African American men, need to stop playing and get serious about our future. I was once told as a teen we needed more real businessmen than "Bidness men!" The difference is a businessman has a card, tax I.D. number, employees, etc. He creates opportunities for himself, his family, and the community. A "businessman" just has a front to make him look good. No credit card, no tax I.D. number, no employees, no nothing. Only his friends that know nothing are also pushing a similar facade. This as men, fathers, husbands, we need to change first. Mawiyah Kambou said, "How can we expect these people to provide any information that might lead to the health, welfare, and development of the African people. We cannot await a people who have denied our reality and attempted to destroy and neutralize the healthiness of our future to provide solutions. We cannot look to these people to restore our way, nor can we consider that they are capable of providing us with the means to do so." We have to become independent! How can we speak on change or a revolution? When we cannot coexist without her help. We must learn to feed ourselves, bank ourselves, clothe ourselves, learning ourselves. We also must start spending our money with people of the same cause, future, and if so, community. We need action, self-reliance, and the vision of a better self. Then a better future will get clear to you. My uncle once told me. "If you get no happiness out of the earth, it is not blamable to God. It is because of your interference to your own happiness." You have to add to your functions as a man first! Learn to be one with yourself, God, and know you play a bigger part in God's intelligent plan. You are the descendant of Kings, Rulers and Warriors. You have to know yourself! Your bloodline is not just slaves. You have to know that leadership, bloodline, and culture mean everything! Why not give it the proper respect to learn yours. Because your ancestors gave pain, blood, and death to get you here, you surely can give a little time.

You have to believe in yourself, first knowing that we are also human beings capable of acting like any other race. Yet, we are still here, standing under greater or worse circumstances. We possess the same intelligence. Still, most don't know the African man. The African man has been sleeping in America for centuries. Marcus Garvey said, "Africans will be favored by the building of this African state because when this state exists. They will be considered and respected as decedents of their powerful country, which has enough to protect them." We as men must realize that the dependence is upon us our destiny, our future is waiting, we must visualize and create that future with a purpose. We must teach each other the way and then learn how to prevent our enemies from establishing orders in our lives, neighborhoods, and countries. Stop the Internal injustices and prejudices in ourselves, sabotaging and dealing your way to progress. This plight will be strenuous and continuous, yet it is all for the purpose of building a stronger you and your family than community. One of my favorite freedom fighters, Mr. Marcus Garvey, said, "I believe that the American Africans have helped to establish the North American civilization, therefore, have a perfect right to live in the U. S, and to aspire to equality of opportunities and treatment of our people." If given the opportunity, we will be great. With this greatness, this desire, we will rise above this environment in another hundred years shall have laid the pillars of the Greatest Civilization the world would have ever seen.

Historically speaking, we have to be ready! Why? Because historically, what goes around comes around, not even in a biblical science but historically and scientifically. The same way the world invaded Africa, these kingdoms have been invaded. Think Greece, Italy, Spain, Persia, etc. I ask you plainly as a Black American who is next. Let me tell you, if only the Black American male change for unity and love, the great United States is next. Don't believe me, just look at the USA today. We as males have to train ourselves, better ourselves, family, children, wives, brothers, and sisters. Teach them how to live better financially, spiritually, and culturally. Then we will see a deeper and better solution. Then we will see a change. We as African Americans don't need financial reparation; I mean, a lot would disagree. I strongly feel that the only reparations we truly need are a reorganization for the crimes committed to our people. Then we will rebuild ourselves.

WOMAN

"We should produce a caliber of young people who can take on the loneliness of struggle that Traditional Africans did not do with leaving things to chance they planned them."

John Heinrick Clark

One of my favorite musicians Mr. Sizzla, a Rastafarian artist. Had an album called" Black Woman and Child" There was a song on that album called "Love is Devine," and in that song, he sang the lyrics like a letter to the princess of Ethiopia? He spoke about having a Black Queen and the joy of their love. In the song, he spoke highly of African love, and today I pray I only get the same point across because I love and respect all women, not just Black.

To the Black American Woman in 2020. The Black man needs you! The Black child needs you; your sisters, mothers, fathers, communities, aunts, uncles, cousins need you! Still, most importantly, you need you. The African American Woman has been bred like cattle in the United States. They have been medically tested, mentally tested, and mistreated by our government for far too long. They have been hated because of their style, uniqueness, and greatness also. She has been raped, sold, marketed, tortured, and disregarded alongside the Blackman. This we must not forget. She has suffered in most cases worse than the male, yet she kept a strong power. She held her strong grace, her strong intelligence, and her African love. Still, the Black woman needs to demand more from themselves and more from their men!

Demand more meaning, holding themselves in a higher regard, respectfully moving as a Queen. Mentally having a Queens values and standards. We live in a time where the Black Man is compelled to be a thug. We live in a time where Black women are compelled to show off their bodies instead of showing off their knowledge, grace, and mental possibilities. The Black woman today is still promoted, marketed as promiscuous and a sex fiend. This needs to change! I admit the Black man has not helped in changing the stereotype. This is why I stated earlier the man needs to start first. We have to give the women something to build on, a strong foundation to start on! The Black woman has to challenge herself for change also. Just as the Black male, she sits atop of a disastrous list that weakens them morally, financially, and educationally. We have to change the fact that 75% of single parents are Black women, 57% of new HIV, AIDS cases are Black women, from the age of 25 -34 years old. Black women are second in teenage pregnancy, only behind the Hispanic females whose culture involves young brides. Only 29% of African American women are married; the rest are left most likely to raise their children alone. This, I feel, is a Dual Parent Problem! Black women, you need to learn to love yourself. Start a family the right way, marriage, then children. Atlanta, GA has one of the highest rates for African American women; they also have one of the highest rates for those women to be lesbians. Don't get me wrong, whatever a person does sexually is on them, yet the male is again abandoned. Is it also a coincidence that most of those missing Black men in Georgia are incarcerated. Georgia has one of the highest rates for African American male incarceration. So yes, I understand that the male is in high shortage due to a racist judicial system and a host of other plots to kill off the Black man. Therefore, it is less to choose from. Also, most are fake thugs who do not need a chance to lead a Black Queen. I have always told my sister and daughters the same. They have to learn to be independent yet find a man who matches their goals, ambitions, and dreams. Then have children. The Black woman has to know that education is a large part of their change. Black women have to be more knowledgeable of themselves. Their past and that knowledge will guide her to a better future.

In 2020 you can look on the internet at any social media platform, and all you see mostly are young Black women in tight revealing clothes or no clothes at all. They are only promoting a stereotype that they could and should be battling differently. We need more graduation, promotional celebration pictures, and less club pictures. The system markets your daughters, sisters, and mothers to be seductive sex-crazed, and they agree to all for a like or a sexist comment. This is no good! The Black woman plays a major role In or fight for equality, in or fight for greatness. In a perfect world where our daughters, sisters, mothers, aunts, and grandmothers are no trapped, molested, human trafficked, prostituted, or filmed to fill a sexual male mentality.

Things would be easier in a world where 57% of sexual predators are White men. Why are Black women #1 in all fields of victims of sexual crimes? Out of respect for my Black women, I will honestly admit I don't know the depths of their pain, mental issues, physical issues etc. I have never lived as a Black woman in America, so I don't know how that feels. I have only lived as a Black man in America. My perception, understanding of a family structure showed me that Black women are strong, undeniable, irreplaceable, and priceless in the world. In Africa, the woman was the strength and focus of the family. She set the standard for her household, children, and husbands. The Queens were the confidants of the villages and helped settle just as many disputes as the King did. They were the ones that taught the younger women culture, spirituality, and how to be a good woman. We have gotten away from that altogether. I remember my grandmother teaching my mother how to cook, sew, quilt, preserve fruits, and do a host of other things. This was her way of passing down culture. Black women are detrimental to the survival of themselves and our culture, children, and Black men. We, as Black men, have to be overstanding and understanding of their specific pains and needs. The pains and need of the chain so slavery. The pains and needs of being fatherless, subjectifies, and extended trust issues etc.

THE WORLD

"We are all human and we have our positive and negative factors those who look for perfection in human are going to be demoralized, frustrate and able to function not realizing that perfection don't exist within themselves. We should strive to develop our strengths and minimize our weaknesses. This requires considerable efforts, but morale will increase as we all accentuate the position and struggle to eliminate the negative."

James Foreman

We as Africans have an untold number of talents; we were the builders of this great nation. We were the bringers of many benefits to this land. We were the founders of agriculture and medicine. So why are we last in both fields now! Africans brought a vast lore of medicines and potions from Africa to the Americas. They learned the use of the local herbs and roots from their own knowledge and the aid of the native Americans with local herbs. Then the slaveowners learned from them. The slaves were used to experiment on also. The great smallpox vaccination, for example. Dr. William Byrd II of Richmond, Virginia, was reportedly recorded, "frequently gave his slaves potions that gave them vomits and purges." He was using them as lab rats, and those treatments were the advancements in the United States medical field.

In Charleston, SC, the nation's first medical teaching hospital, used live slaves for demonstrations and dissections. The father of modern-day gynecology J. Marrow Sims from South Carolina, frequently operated on enslaved women as test subjects. It was said he operated on a slave named Anabell, Lucy, and Betsy. It was said he operated on them some thirty times, sewing their insides without anesthesia. Describing his horrors as medical research! The sickle cell trait is believed to have evolved as a defense against malaria, to which many of the enslaved were immune. With our lives literally, we gave for their advancement medically and financially. We gave everything to this nation and received nothing. Africans have created greatness around this world. We help them change their world. Why not change our world and ourselves. We were detrimental in forging the United States. We aided their revolution; why can't we lead our own? Crispus Attuck was a Black and Indian mix man. He was detrimental in the Boston massacre. He was the first to rally and the first to die.

There can be no growth in oppression, mental or financial without death. Twenty-seven people died making the Brooklyn Bridge, and sixty died building the Empire State Building, sixty thousand died building the Panama canal. Progress is a lot like the war it cost. Millions of slaves died building this country. We have to adjust our own economic present in readiness for the future! In the history of humanity, only two things transcend life, children and art. Most of us aren't artists, so we have to teach our children! Marcus Garvey said, "Confidence! If you have no confidence in yourself, you are twice defeated in the race of life. With confidence, you have won before you have started." As the Black American man must start being productive citizens, fathers, husbands, and men first!

We have to create a food corridor and start producing Black-owned products. Those products being economically controlled by African Americans all the way to our tables. In the United States, African Americans do most of buying products and the best of creating products. Yet, last in selling products. Why is this? Because in the past, we invented, created, imagined. If we marketed our own structural food system, we as a people could first benefit financially, creating a parallel economy first. Healthwise, we can monitor our own products, ensuring that the products are good for our children. Jewish people don't support Jewish businesses just because they are Jewish. They support them because they are trying to help the community financially, their race financially. We as African Americans, don't do that.

Today is 6-04-2020, one of the darkest weeks in the United States. This week I saw Blacks, Whites, Asians, Spanish, Indians, and all mixed races protest and fight for equality against police brutality. I watched the young and the old fight, the straight, lesbians and homosexuals fight! Side by side! The murder of George Floyd sparked a light this week that the White supremacist America didn't expect. The people are tired, and the people are fed up! Black men have suffered in the world for far too long. Has the

African American male not bore the weight of building the United States out of jungles, forests, and swamps. We constructed this great land. We have served without entitlement or payment all to this capitalist, racist system for almost four hundred years. The Black man has contributed his best to America, and now they want your lives and our children's lives. All this fighting amongst ourselves, and we still have not gained equality or Aide for our offspring to live a better life. We just get more smokescreens.

The Black man only wants those things that belong to the Black race. We want real equality in the land we mostly built. We want equality in London, Africa, Brazil, and everywhere else in the world. If only the African Americans had a bond with Africa, an understanding with Africa. Why? Because Africa is ours, to win Africa, we will give up America. Have any of you asked yourselves in 2020 why is China buying up Africa right now? "This rush for territory, this encroachment on land is only a desire of the strong nations especially the White race to get a hold of those portions of land necessary for their economic existence, knowing well, that in two hundred years. There will not be enough supply in the world for all its inhabitants. At present, the weaker people must die, the Africans are the weakest people, and if we do not get power and strength, we shall be doomed to extermination." Marcus Garvey said this a long time ago; either he was a psychic or just was on the right path. I go with the latter. We have to commit action, self-reliance. The vision of self and the future have to be clear to you. If you will think and compare the future possibilities within America, you must understand Africa's past first! Then you will understand that there is no salvation for Africans in America. Still, with a free independent Africa with a better social system, they could help American

Africans. Then together, we could/might have a chance. We have to know who we are first and that you cannot If you don't know your past! We don't have to go there just to start commerce and trade with our own kind! We then could be the masters of our own fate!

The Africans have to organize globally because racism is a global problem. We have to teach the youth, raise our children in positive environments. We have to be grateful for the gift of education cause once upon a time, you would be castrated and amputated if you got caught trying to read! Castrated so you couldn't produce children, so I urge all Black men to reproduce! Reproduce in the correct manner, though, reproduce to be a father, leader, and pass on positive knowledge. As parents, most African families worry about all the wrong things, clothes, and shoes etc. All kinds of bullshit! Why we don't worry about their true education. The owners of these brands don't worry because we are foolishly putting their kids through school. We have to change our way of parenting to produce a better and smarter generation.

Racism is a power system that is globally accepted. The system means to control someone's destiny and life. Racism is different from hate; it takes political, financial, economic resources to employ racism. If a person hates a person, or a people were calling them nigger or coon etc. That is called being prejudice, not racism. I once read an African proverb that said, "I am not what you call me; I am what I respond to." Therefore, if you want to be treated as men, women stop calling each other niggas, bitches, hoes, etc. If we want to be recognized by the world and treated in this world as men, then we have to act like men. It amazes me that most of the biggest racists don't even know their history. Before they even knew who they were, we

Break the Chains

knew how they were. Before the 1500's Caucasians were not classified as White, Caucasians stated they were Italian, Greek, Russian, etc. All until Carl Lan Yonas and Yohan Prima Blomingback started writing books on Arian supremacy, thus sparking the Aryan interest. Even today, they are considered the father of White supremacy. It has been since the Catholic church gave the Portuguese authority to take the slaves out of Africa. It has been since the transatlantic slave trade started.

White supremacy has not stopped trying to degrade, oppress and force an economical imprisonment on African Americans. So, I ask you why we should stop in the pursuit to free our brothers that are still in bondage, imprisonment, and servitude. They didn't take a break, so why should we take a break on freeing ourselves, brothers, and sisters. If we must correct this madman structure of the state and apply the corporate majesty of the people for their own good, then we must reach the source. Then reorganize and reform our way of thinking, living, and educating ourselves. We have to change the way we treat each other, communicate with each other. I've always heard that your five closest friends will determine who you are. We need to change who we are, who we associate with, what we watch, listen to and promote. Music was once how Blacks told story's and communicated. Its been times in Black history in America where we were beaten or killed for beating drums and singing in America. Why? Because with those songs, we would sing, told stories of oppression and escape. Even today, the youth do this, yet the mainstream can't see the message. How could you not see the pain in Tupac "This White Man World" or Ice Cube "Today was a Good Day." They are only beating the drums telling the story of oppression, police brutality, imprisonment, and bondage in this foreign land!

The Black race's future lies heavily on our blood and in our blood. The fight that laid in Nazinga An Shaka's blood lays in your blood. The persistence of education that Malcolm X had lays in your blood. The Africans had to rise to meet the restrictions and freedom of the future. We must realize that the dependencies on us, our destiny, our future are waiting. We must visualize and create that future, that Utopia, that Wakanda as to speak. First, we must teach each other the way, and then we must keep learning together. Thus, preventing our enemies from establishing order again in our lives. We must change our neighborhood and communities for the better if not, they will infiltrate your great deeds with injustices and prejudices to derail the progress. We must never forget the pursuit of progress is long. Never forget the North American Indian who has been almost exterminated to make room for the American White man, and he never cried when we were hung, shot, overdosed, raped, or mass incarcerated. He never helped as they enslaved our minds, body, and soul. So why would we look for him to help now!

LAST THOUGHTS

A man can only testify to the range of his vision! Let me ask you a question. Would you ever ask a medical doctor's opinion on how to fix a car? Any knowledgeable person wouldn't, knowing he has no knowledge in that field. Picture it vice versa, and your answer would still be no! Again "A man can only testify to the range of his vision." So, I ask the reader who is better suited to write a book on the pains of chains of slavery's imprint than a person that has lived through an inadequate educational system, a life of crime, imprisonment, and change for the better, who I ask, other than a person that has survived this and lived to tell it. Yes, I ran the streets of America, running a criminal organization. I dealt with drugs, guns, money, etc. I served time for those mistakes and, during that solace, that mental isolation. I learned my history, my morals, my culture. I learned what they didn't teach or what they didn't want me to learn. Again no one in their right mind will take advice from a person not studied or experienced in that field. We have learned as humans how to evolve, grow, and change. I walked thru the racial fires of the United States system's racial traps. Traps of prison, drug use and sales. I've lived the wrong life of a criminal. Walked in housing projects from Florida to New York. Then one day, I asked myself the questions of life, racial equality, police brutality, spiritually and culturally. I didn't view sematic racism from the skybox. I viewed it from the playing field!

Let me ask you one last question. Have you ever seen a soul food restaurant in China Town or a Chinese neighborhood, Italian neighborhood? Let me answer that for you. NO! If it were ever one, they would have gone out of business. That question was meant for a joke, yet it is very real, and most don't give it the thought that it deserves. Still, there is a Chinese restaurant, Pizzeria's, all over Black neighborhood not only are they feeding you unhealthy food. They are economically playing a big role in a systematic bias system. Example: You have two male boys one is White, his name is John, the other Black name Jay. Because John's father owns a business in the Black neighborhoods, he has had money and White privilege and passed down ex-slave money all his life. He is able to raise John in a good neighborhood. While Jay's father has been incarcerated falsely for drugs for years, he and his family have barely survived. The public schools rely on property tax mostly to fund the schools in the community. So, John's school is a million times better than Jay's. Jay's school has old books, old programs, computers, etc. They have over-filled classrooms, no SAT prep, a list of other problems. John's school has everything new a tennis court, soccer, a polo team, the classes are small, and the school a lot safer and cleaner. After this, John still gets an extra boost. John is not worried about his Senior year because his dad has money set aside for his college while Jay is busy applying for student loans. After college, Jay has no loans to pay back, enabling him to buy a house or small business. While student loans hold Jay back more and more, keeping him behind. This is systematic racism! How do you think Jay will make it out of this area without help. Systematic racism is done with wealth, incarceration, education, political representation, and many other ways. How do we solve a systematic problem? Easy with systematic solutions! For years we have let them take! For years we have let them slave us and make billions of dollars in economics out of our communities and put nothing in them. I see you shaking your heads, yet most African Americans still accept this as just a reality or just apart from being Black. That's crazy! That is not reality, and it's a system that is against your survival, existence, education and bloodline. I again am only here beating the drum sounding the alarm of the slaves. I said it before; I know why the caged bird sings. These are actual times I have experienced, a lesson in my life and history. When I grew mentally, my ambitions grew also. That is how I can testify to the cages meaning and restraints because I have been ignorant before, blinded living in the matrix, so to speak or living a street life. Not to glorify that lifestyle, only again showing you what lead to the transformation in my life. Thinking and writing. That path led to me writing "Break the Chains" That struggle lead me to seek the knowledge, understanding and heritage of my bloodline. I found pride in who I have been and soon to become.

 I don't consider myself to be the most knowledgeable man on this planet on these subjects because I have no degree. It was all self-taught hunger by living through the smokescreens and systems. We have all lived under that pressure, yet instead of letting it crack you. Let that pressure turn you into a diamond. Marcus Garvey said, "Many a man was educated outside the schoolroom. It's is something you let out, not completely take in. You are part of it, for it is natural." I learned I grew and transformed myself into a seeker of knowledge. The same knowledge my ancestors fought for me to have. I want it! Then like most humans before me, after gaining knowledge, it is your obligation to inform others. I felt a fire to tell my story to the world. When asked why my reply will always be because it is mine, it is unlike no one else. I felt obligated to my children, family, community, bloodline to tell my story. I owed the world! I had to share my evolution, my pain and my knowledge. No matter what the criticism I receive from this book, I am personally satisfied and feel my job as a Blackman in 2021 is almost complete. I want you, the reader, to stay vigilant, prayerful, and seeking. We have to keep hunting knowledge. Stay hungry, my brother and sister, and walk with morals, strength, and pride!

ABOUT THE AUTHOR

Pachino Allen Williams was born December 21, 1979, in Atlanta, GA. He comes from a big family. His father had nine brothers and sisters. His grandfather was a sharecropper in Thomasville, GA. His mother had seven sisters and a brother, and her mother was an evangelist in Tampa, FL. Pachino's family filled his ears with tales of slavery, oppression, and Black pride. His uncle Dr. Larry Spruill is an accomplished author and college history professor. His uncles had a public broadcasting show in Tampa about Black politics and struggle on his mother's side. His brother Shannon Williams, cousins Miriam Williams and Rachel Paten are also accomplished authors. Pachino was a good student, yet he got into a little trouble growing up like most boys. He graduated high school in 1998 and joined the military were, and he left after a year on an honorable discharge. From 2001 to 2010, Pachino ran a record label/criminal organization.

In 2010 he was convicted of manslaughter because someone tried to rob him at his recording studio in College Park, GA Pachino served years at a maximum-security prison. Pachino was a self-taught writer and wrote a couple of novels. "Confessions of a kingpin," "Diamonds and Dollars," and a self-help book called "The Art of the Hustler" Before writing "Break The Chains. Pachino has four children Samaria Emani, Jahhlive, and Kayla. He has dedicated his life to changing the lives of his family, people of color, and poverty.

REFERENCES

1. "THE NEW JIM CROW" Michelle Alexander
2. " BLACK PROPHETIC FIRE" Dr. Cornell West
3. "UNFINISHED NATION" Alan Brinkley
4. "SLAVERY BY ANOTHER NAME" Douglas A. Blackmon
5. "BEFORE THE MAYFLOWER" Lerone Bennet Jr.
6. "ASAFO" Mwalimu K. Bomani Baruti
7. "DESTRUCTION OF BLACK CIVILIZATION" Chancellor Williams
8. "MALCOLM X" Alex Haley
9. "DARKWARTER" W.E.B. Dubois
10. "AFRICAN FUNDUMENTALISM" Marcus Garvey
11. "EMANCIPATION FROM MENTAL SLAVERY" Marcus Garvey
12. "THE MAKING OF A SLAVE" Willie Lynch
13. "THEY CAME BEFORE COLUMBUS" Ivan Van Sertima
14. "THE AMERICAN SLAVE COAST" Ned & Constance Sublette
15. " BLACK INDIANS" William Loren Katz
16. "FROM BABYLON TO TIMBUKTU" Rudolph R Windsor
17. "THE HISTORY OF THE NEGRO CHURCH" Carter G. Wilson

www.ingramcontent.com/pod-product-compliance
Lightning Source LLC
Chambersburg PA
CBHW071446070526
44578CB00001B/236